Steep Terrain

Steep Terrain

BY

CONTENTS

1. Howling Mad — 1
2. Boom — 13
3. Rescues — 25
4. Beef It Up — 33
5. Marooned — 45
6. Tragic Accident — 59
7. Trouble — 65
8. Widowmaker — 75
9. Frozen Stiff — 83
10. Nothing But Rubble — 91
11. Animals of a Different Kind — 97

CONTENTS

12 | Reverend Vincent Price 113
13 | The Bottom Scratcher 119
14 | Steel Armadillo 133
15 | Bouncy Houses 143
16 | What Hump? 153
17 | The Dangers of Being a Kid 163
18 | The Plane from Hell 177
19 | A Miracle 183
20 | International Cases 191
21 | Tragedy 199
22 | Conjoined Twins 205
23 | Cats that Need Fixin' 211
24 | A Daughter's Hero 223

ACKNOWLEDGEMENTS 231
ABOUT THE AUTHOR 235

For my dad

Copyright © 2022 by Brichelle Young

All rights reserved. No part of this book may be reproduced in any manner whatsoever without written permission except in the case of brief quotations embodied in critical articles and reviews.

First Printing, 2022

Alta Helicopter
University of Utah Archives

1

Howling Mad

I was hooked. It was a world my dad painted in my mind while I sat on a fluffy rug at his feet. The tales of days long past, woven together like a tapestry of muddy medical tape and unstable household chemicals. He relaxed into the couch, surrounded by four walls of bare logs, each beam a different size and shape and having been stripped of its bark by hand. The cathedral ceiling held a red, metal roof that played a symphony during rainstorms and cracked thunder when releasing a heavy blanket of snow. Mexican terracotta tiles lined the floor, washed in sandy hues, and several had imprints of dog paws where a four-legged visitor had taken a jog through the factory yard. The stone fireplace was our perfect cure on a cold winter night, and amongst the ashes were remnants of last year's Christmas wrapping paper. The home was too large to be called a cabin but too small to be a log home. Our house fell somewhere in between.

My dad's stories captivated me from an early age and lit my imagination with possibilities. I sat there in our living room, hanging onto each word as he told me of a trip to the snow-covered Ruby Mountains of Elko, Nevada. The situation resembled a scene from the over-the-top action TV series, *The A-Team*. At the time, my dad was a young ski patrolman from Alta, Utah, and had been invited to this up-and-coming ski resort and was given complimentary ski passes in exchange for drumming up springtime business when most people started thinking about golf. Happy to embark on a free ski trip, he was now doubting his choices and worried he might not live to see another day.

My dad, Lynn Falkner, found himself strapped into a helicopter and racing straight for the clouds. He caught a glimpse over his shoulder where his two buddies, and fellow Alta ski patrolmen, were gripping their seats and praying they'd make it off this chopper alive. This French-made Lama was the most indomitable helicopter of its time and was capable of reaching elevations as high as the summit of Mount Everest. Its spindly frame held an engine directly under the rotors with a bulb on the front where the four-man group was encased. The machine was designed for extreme altitudes, which was exactly where they were headed.

With the helicopter's nose pointing to space, they ascended higher and higher at a blood-curdling speed. Lynn glanced at the pilot, who must surely have a death wish, and saw the man's wide-eyed grin that screamed, "This is what I live for!" Lynn turned forward to the infinite sky rushing toward him and shielded his eyes from the sun's piercing glare. Suddenly, the chopper lost momentum, and Lynn felt the G-force release its pressure from his body. The engine coughed and stalled into a heart-gripping silence. As the ascent came to a halt, Lynn felt his heart lift into his throat but wasn't sure if it was caused by the weightlessness or the heart-stopping fear. He then felt his stomach lift into his chest as the helicopter began to free-fall out of the sky. Lynn glanced back at the pilot, hoping the man would come to his senses, and heard the roar of air rush past as they plummeted toward Earth. Lynn and his buddies were scared witless.

....

Lynn grew up in Utah's Wasatch mountains, a world-class mecca for deep powder skiing. The bright sun that bounced off the winter snow darkened the countless freckles on his face and made them even more pronounced above his full 1970s mustache. A man of moderate stature, he proudly maintained Hulk-like thigh muscles, a benefit of spending every day careening down mountain slopes.

Alta was only one of three resorts in the United States that restricted its customers to skiers. While Lynn had no prejudice against snowboarders, he did enjoy the occasional joke at their expense. He had become an experienced skier long before joining the patrol, but only on the smooth slopes carefully maintained by the resort. Once he joined the team, he had to learn how to ski off the beaten path. "I couldn't just look good shaking my legs going down a groomed hill," he said. "I had to learn how to handle the deep and the steep and the powder and the trees."

He hadn't joined the patrol for the modest wage it paid; he joined for the girls. He loved helping them on the slopes and being their white knight when they needed aid. Then, after a long day's work, he enjoyed hangin' with the boys, since only men were allowed on the team at the time. His love of adventure made him a natural addition, and the team quickly took to him with his lightheartedness and humor. Other perks of the job included a set of skis and free season passes to the "Greatest Snow on Earth." It was a dream job for a young adventurer like Lynn, and he was being paid in powder.

As a patrolman, Lynn's job focused entirely on skier safety. His first week was spent training in emergency medicine and earning certifications in Outdoor Emergency Care and Mountain Travel and Rescue. He learned how to perform first aid in the wilderness, strap injured skiers onto bright orange rescue toboggans, and carefully pull them down the mountain.

....

Back in the Ruby Mountains, Lynn had piloted his patrol buddies down from Salt Lake City in his own five-seater plane. After an uneventful flight, they landed at a small, regional airport in Elko. While refueling the plane's tank, Lynn approached the attendant at the hangar. "Where will the helicopter for heli-skiing come in?"

"It lands outside the city," the man answered. "It's a ranching community called Lamoille. The pilot picks up his passengers behind the bar there. He doesn't come out here."

Lynn sighed at what must have been a miscommunication with the resort when, suddenly, the "poof-poof-poof-" of whirling rotor blades was heard, and a helicopter came into view.

"I've never seen this happen before," the attendant said.

As the craft swept in, Lynn and his two patrol buddies grabbed their gear and jumped on board the Lama. They shook hands with the pilot, who introduced himself and said, "Let's go skiing." Lynn and the other patrolmen were not paying customers, so the pilot knew he had free reign to mess with them. The speed of the rotors surged as the man opened up the throttle and lifted them into the air.

"This thing's got some power behind it!" Lynn called over from the adjacent seat.

"You think so?" he smiled. "Watch this."

The pilot thrust the chopper forward into a series of whiplash-inducing twists and climbs. As they dropped down over the canyon floor, perilously close to the spruce and whitebark pine trees, Lynn thought the skids were going to knock tufts of needles right off the tops. They shot across the base of the landscape, and Lynn couldn't see what lay at the edge of the forest, but the pilot seemed to have it memorized and could probably fly it blind. Suddenly, the trees came to an abrupt halt, and the chopper took a nosedive down the sheer side of a cliff. He was thrust up from his seat as they plunged toward the canyon below, but he gripped onto his latched seatbelt, knowing it was the only thing keeping him from flying out the open door.

Lynn was reminded of the heli-pilot back at Alta, whom everyone called LC, short for "Lucky Chuck." A gutsy man himself, he could fly with the best of them, but today this Elko pilot was going to give LC a run for his money. The man began a series of sharp up and down arches as if on a rollercoaster track, dropping them into a steep dive to gain as much speed as possible.

Once Lynn thought they had reached terminal velocity, the pilot pulled up and they began climbing for the sky once more. At this point, Lynn expected the pilot to plateau for a few moments of zero-G weightlessness but was surprised to find the man had a much more terrifying idea in mind.

Instead of leveling out, he held the chopper in a vertical position and let the engine stall. The moment the engine cut out so did Lynn's heart. They began to tumble out of the sky as Lynn felt his seatbelt pulling him toward the canyon below. Lynn watched desperately as the pilot turned the engine over and got the rotors spinning. They regained control just before Lynn's premonition of crashing into the rocks became a reality. He gave an audible sigh of relief as the flight mellowed into a steady course for their mountain top destination, and he knew he'd soon be on the ground.

"Have you ever heard of LC?" Lynn asked. "He's our pilot back home at Alta." At the mention of the name, the Elko pilot lowered his head in a mixture of defeat and admiration. "He's the best," he replied.

Once their helicopter skids set down on the white, crunchy snow, the wobbly patrolmen clambered out of the cockpit, grasping their skis and poles. They were relieved to be back in their natural habitat and excited to be spending the rest of the day cutting waves of snow into the air as they slalomed down the hillside. Each time Lynn and his buddies reached the mountain's base, they jumped back on the Lama, but were grateful to be returned to the top without the theatrics of the first flight. Some of the drop-off points were too steep for the chopper to set both skids down, so the pilot delicately balanced one skid on the snow while the skiers jumped out. As Lynn peered across the horizon and gazed at the rugged snow-capped mountains, he felt like he was at the top of the world.

The first morning after returning home to the Alta Ski Resort, Lynn stepped from the warm patrol house and into the dark, frosty air. The blackness of the early hours was broken only by a few small lights along the roofline. Before heading up the mountain to fulfill his avalanche duties, Lynn and his fellow patrolmen trudged over to the Buckhorn for some grub. It was more like a military chow hall than a restaurant, and served only the early-rising Alta employees, such as the patrol and lift crew. It came with a cook who could be likened to a czar, and, when Lynn walked in wrapped from head to toe in winter clothes, the man yelled, "Take your hat off! No soup for you!" Regardless of the hospitality, or lack thereof, Lynn revered the pancakes, eggs, and little sausages everyone called "poodledinks."

After a second helping of the piping hot poodledinks, Lynn and the crew cleaned up their plates and headed back outside. Fat snowflakes drifted down as they marched toward the powder cache building to raid the resort's supply of explosives. Other than the crunching of their boots, the crisp air was still and quiet, as if daring someone to make a noise. Lynn stepped inside the small building and pulled three hand charges off a shelf, each weighing two pounds and resembling a can of homemade chili. He grabbed two extra for good measure and tucked them inside his blue patrol jacket marked with the Alta insignia over an embroidered large, white snowflake. Lynn remembered the heavy snowfall they had received over the last few days and smiled, thinking of how deep the powder must be.

The sharp, jagged peaks that punched skyward from the valley floor formed a breathtaking landscape. The elevation, steep terrain, and significant snowfall made the skiing here first class. However, it also made the job of a ski patrolman significantly more difficult. Every member of the patrol had a heavy sense of respect for Mother Nature and knew that looking for signs of avalanche danger was essential to maintaining safety in the canyon. It wasn't just skiers who were in danger, but anyone and anything, including lodges, apartment buildings, homes, and cars.

The highway that traveled up from the Salt Lake Valley, through Little Cottonwood Canyon, and to the resort maintains significant and unique challenges. Along its nine-mile length, it crosses sixty-five avalanche paths, several of which are serious hot spots for danger. The canyon is extremely narrow and has one of the highest avalanche indexes in the world. Eighty percent of the structures at Alta are within an avalanche run-off zone, and the threats constantly keep the patrol on their toes. Their goal is to initiate small avalanches before the resort opens each morning to prevent larger, naturally occurring ones that could wipe civilization right out of the canyon.

Members of the patrol are required to use the buddy system, and Lynn's team included Hunter Holmes and Gabe Garcia. When Lynn was hired, he had filled out a green sheet asking which avalanche duties he would prefer. Most men picked the jobs that included the least off-trail skiing and got them back to the warmth of the patrol shack the quickest. Lynn, Hunter, and Gabe preferred the opposite. Skiing off the beaten path and throwing hand charges into the mountainside was what they lived for. Not to mention, Colorado-native Gabe was a deep-powder maniac.

As a few rays of sun crept over the ridge, the trio boarded a ski lift named for the mountain it climbed, Supreme. They were headed for the only place hand charges were allowed to be thrown from a lift chair, a practice that was usually, and understandably, forbidden. As Lynn looked over the treetops, he could see two other patrolmen perched high on the cross structure of a ski lift tower. To make routine repairs, the patrolmen were trained to scale those mighty towers and keep their cool at the top. Any acrophobia had to be left at home because there was no room for a fear of heights on the ski patrol.

"We're almost there. Let's light this baby up," Hunter said. Lynn pulled a small tool from his pocket and handed it to Hunter, who used it to cut the fuse tip off for a clean, dry start. He then slid the ignitor over the blasting cap and lit the fuse with a good yank, starting the clock. But instead of throwing the charge immediately, Hunter tossed it to Lynn. Clutching a ticking time bomb, Lynn promptly tossed it back. It went back and forth in a game of hot potato until Lynn felt the game had gone on too long and called uncle, throwing it as far as he could onto the hillside. Without a moment to spare, the explosion released a concussive force that hit them as they hung there, slowly being carried up the mountain. This wasn't the first time they played that game and it wouldn't be the last.

Still swaying in their lift chairs, Lynn watched as the resort helicopter came into view, thrusting gusts of air downward and blowing swirls of snow off a ridge. The chopper swooped over them and headed for the remote areas of the resort where the anti-avalanche cannons couldn't reach. Lynn was never assigned a job onboard a helicopter, but often caught a ride during recreational skiing. He watched the chopper as two small bombs were tossed out the door, free-falling onto a particularly steep ridge and detonating into an eruption of snow and smoke. Lynn never tired of watching explosions of snow burst into the sky, which was made even more beautiful with a backdrop that resembled an oil painting.

On their way down through the back trails of the mountain, Lynn, Gabe, and Hunter cut through powder deep enough to sweep over them like a wave. Even though it made visibility impossible at times, it was well worth the natural high. When they reached the base, the trio stopped to check on the rest of the guys, and Lynn marched sideways up a small hill to a tower where his buddies, Stuart Thompson and Jim Head, stood. It was the 1970's and most of the guys sported mustaches, including Lynn, but Stuart carried his bushy 'stache exceptionally well. As a cowboy from Wyoming, it was in his heritage. Stuart was the main man in charge of the artillery because his time in the Army had given him invaluable experience. Long after he retired from Alta, he continued to train the new patrolmen on proper handling and safety. In many ways, Alta was the wild west, but not with avalanche control.

Lynn clipped off his skies and climbed the ladder to check their progress. It was usually a short climb, but the length of the ladder depended on the height of the snowdrifts that day, and the tower needed to be high enough that even prized levels of Rocky Mountain snowfall couldn't bury it. Between Stuart and Jim sat a piece of artillery with an exceptionally long and skinny barrel pointing high in the sky. This was a nitrogen-compressed cannon called an "Avalauncher," a standard piece of weaponry found at ski resorts worldwide. Stuart opened the base of the barrel, slipped in a two-pound explosive projectile, and then cranked the pressure from the air tank. "All set!" he called over his shoulder. He didn't need to take the time to aim because avalaunchers are pre-set to specific target coordinates, making them useful even in whiteout conditions.

As he hit the firing mechanism and the bomb launched into the air, blue flames shot from the barrel, and the sound of a "thwip" was heard. They watched as the bomb hit the mountain and detonated into a shower of snow and rock. Lynn waited for the sound of the explosion to reach them, reminding him of thunderstorms when he would spot a bolt of lightning and count how many seconds passed before he heard the thunder. The farther away he was from the target, the longer it took for the sound to reach him.

Eliminating the avalanche danger often required more than one bomb in any given area. Lynn could see the ridge where they were targeting and noticed the blanket of snow was relatively unmoved, so Stuart loaded the canon again and shot three more bombs. The last one did the trick, triggering a slide of packed snowfall and a few rocks to come rolling down the hill. However, Alta kept much bigger guns than the Avalauncher in their battle against nature.

2

Boom

The next morning, Lynn caught a ride up the Wildcat lift to the resort's heaviest piece of artillery. On loan from the military, the howitzer cannon was a gnarly machine that looked like it had been ripped off the top of a tank. Although not as long as the avalauncher, the howitzer's barrel was much beefier in diameter, and the forceful blast was right out of the movies. When Lynn was working with it, he felt like he was in a real war. A couple of patrolmen, including Stuart, stood next to it while wearing heavy-duty hearing protection. They would need it.

"Hang on, I gotta take a leak," one of the guys said, heading over to a patrol shack found at the top of the lift. As Lynn watched him climb the ladder and walk in, he waited for the moment a stream of pee would come trickling out onto the snow below. Inside each shack was a PVC pipe sticking up out of the floor, specifically for peeing in. Outside on the ground below was a perpetual circle of frozen, yellow snow. Years later, when women started joining the team, these pipes were deemed inappropriate and removed.

As soon as the man returned, another patrolman called "Hambone" lifted a massive shell from under the platform and heaved it up to Stuart at the canon. These charges, ordered from WWII stockpiles, were a far cry from the ones used by the avalaucher and looked like the heat shields often seen wrapped around semi-truck exhaust stacks. Hambone, whose full name was Hamilton George Strayer III, was a tall man with a serious demeanor despite his knack for bold unpredictability. As Hambone passed off the artillery shell, Stuart loaded it into the howitzer and gave a nod.

"Here goes!" Jim Head called out, and everyone clutched their hearing protection tight to their ears.

"FIRE!" Stuart pulled the rope-like trigger and turned his head to shield himself from the deafening blast of the discharge.

"BOOM!" The bomb shot out of the barrel and headed straight for an especially heavy-laden peak. Howitzers are often mounted on a set of wheels, allowing them to lurch forward and spring back upon firing, but this was a recoilless 105. Much like the avalauncher, its fixed position and secure mount meant it could repeat trajectories without having to be recalibrated. Lynn watched as the charge sailed toward the ridge and detonated before hitting the mountain, allowing the explosive wave to impact a larger area. The "KA-BOOM!" of the blast rippled through the canyon, and a flood of snow came pouring down the canyon wall.

STEEP TERRAIN

Avalanche Control
University of Utah Archives

On another morning of avalanche rounds, Lynn, Titus, and their boss, Piney, were on Mount Baldy when a couple of other patrolmen were crossing the ridge above them and accidentally pushed off an avalanche. Lynn and Piney managed to skirt to the side and find safety out of the damage path, but Titus attempted to cheat death by springing off the trail and into a tree like a rabbit. He dug his skis into the trunk for extra grip and held on as the avalanche passed around him. The wave of snow was not deep enough to swallow him, but it cleared a path right down to the dirt. When it was all over, they found several car-sized boulders at the bottom and realized Titus had been a very lucky man.

It wasn't all business at Alta, and pulling pranks on Snowbird became as much a sport as skiing was. During Christmas, Alta took a box of donuts to Snowbird's patrol in an apparent gesture of goodwill. The men happily accepted and fully consumed the confections, completely unaware of the secret they were hiding. Before they had handed over the donuts, Alta had taken a photo of them, but they weren't displayed in a box. Instead, each was held on the patrolmen's naked genitals, with some even "up the dog's tail."

Alta patiently sat on the photo until April Fool's Day the next spring, and then gave it to the Snowbird lift crew to ensure the evidence wouldn't get buried the minute it was handed over. As the Snowbird patrol boarded the tram that morning, the lift crew eagerly slipped them the photo and watched as they reeled in horror. As hoped, the lift crew teased them mercilessly. That photo still exists today but is kept under a tight seal. No patrolman I've spoken with has dared release it, especially to me, Lynn's daughter.

On another April Fool's Day, Alta used a snowcat driver who worked both resorts to sneak a dud into the lion's den. The driver placed the explosive in the snow next to the patrol office, but the joke was taken more seriously than intended. The resort was placed on emergency lockdown and an explosives crew was brought in to dispose of the shell. Luckily, it was early in the morning and before the day's customers would arrive, minimizing any loss of income. As the bomb squad inspected the charge, they realized it was hollow, and inside found a note that read, "April Fools! Haha! Jokes on you." After that, the Alta patrol found themselves in hot water, but they remained undeterred.

Both Alta and Snowbird maintained their own newspapers, but, for one April Fool's Day, Alta managed to replicate the Snowbird edition and fill it with sensationalized stories of finding dead bodies and selling things from the resort. They distributed the papers to various Snowbird lodges, and it took a while before the local residents realized they were fake.

The pranks were far from a one-way street as Snowbird enjoyed the games as much as Alta did. To seek revenge for the bomb scare, Snowbird took a dummy and hung it by a rope off the steep cliffs of their shared mountain, Mount Baldy. As the sunrise crept over the horizon, one of Lynn's buddies stood on the deck of the patrol house and peered through a pair of binoculars. Lynn stepped out to see what was going on when the man casually reported, "Snowbird's just playing an April first joke. We can all go back to sleep." The fruitless attempt at payback fizzled and died.

On another occasion, Alta put up its annual display of plastic flamingoes in front of the resort's ski shop, The Powder House. Once the pink birds were happily roosting out front, they mysteriously disappeared, and the only evidence left at the scene was a carefully crafted note. Created using letters cut from a magazine, it looked like something made by a serial killer. To prove the note was from the thief, a piece of plastic had been carved off one of the flamingoes and taped to the paper. No one could figure out who had committed the kidnapping or where the birds had gone. The flamingoes weren't seen again until springtime when they re-appeared on a float in the Alta parade. The patrolmen returned the birds to their home at the Powder House, but the culprit was no closer to being identified. One thing the patrol knew for sure was it must have been a member of Alta because Snowbird wasn't that clever.

The rival patrol wasn't Alta's only target, as even their customers were at risk. One particularly warm day, Lynn and a fellow patrolman rode up a lift with a lap full of apples and watched happy skiers enjoying the sunshine. Lynn noticed two ladies cruising the hillside wearing nothing but ski goggles, gloves, and bikinis. This was not an uncommon sight when the weather permitted. As the lift carried them toward a particularly crowded run, they began chewing the apples into a mash and pretended to groan and grab their stomachs. This was their moment. Hyping up the mock nausea, they pretended to vomit and spewed their mashed apple contents over the innocent bystanders below.

"AvaDog"
University of Utah Archives

The patrol kept at least one avalanche search and rescue dog, nicknamed an "Ava-dog," as an invaluable rescue asset when things went wrong. It was usually a German Sheperd, but for one April Fool's Day, a patrolman named Louie took it upon himself to add a new animal to the team.

"I got us a goat!" he proclaimed.

"That's ridiculous," Lynn said. "Where are you even going to keep it?"

"Jonesy is out of town on vacation, so his bunkhouse is available. It's perfect!" This bachelor apartment at Alta would not be vacant for long as its resident, Steve Jones, would be returning soon. After just a week-long absence, he came home to a foul-smelling apartment full of fecal pellets and urine. A professional cleaning crew was called in, but it's doubtful they ever got rid of the pungent smell, and Doug nearly fired Louie over the incident. The goat was no help to the search and rescue team, so they found it a properly suited home and moved on.

While the fun was usually worth the trouble, sometimes there were more uncomfortable consequences to their exploits.

"Hey, Binger," a patrolman whispered. "Get your textbook and meet me in the bathroom."

An Alta patrolman himself, Bill Binger was studying zoology at the University of Utah and, upon his return with the requested resource material, was ushered quickly and quietly around the corner. Once inside the restroom, the man proceeded to lower his ski pants to the top of his pubic hair.

"What do you think these are?" He asked Binger.

By this time, a gathering of patrolmen was craning their heads through the door, including Hambone who weighed in authoritatively. "You don't need that book. He's got the f%&@ crabs!" Sure enough, there on page 247 was a drawing of a critter who looked identical to their object of curiosity, labeled 'Crab Louse.' Panic spread among the other patrollers. They knew they were at risk as well because a group of flight attendants had come through town and cut a fairly wide swath through the patrol ranks. "Thank heavens that's not me," Lynn thought to himself, now with an image forever burned in his mind. When the exposed patrolman asked what he should do about it, he was given an extremely unorthodox answer.

"You know what you've got to do to get rid of them, don't you?" Hambone asked. "Shave off half of your pubic hair, put lighter fluid on the other half, and then light it. When the critters run from the flames, kill them with an ice pick!" Everyone gaped at Hambone because they knew he was dead serious. He was known for having strange ideas, but this was a doozy.

"That's the craziest thing I've ever heard," a patrolman said.

"You should really get that looked at by a doctor," Lynn suggested.

Once the crowd dispersed, the patrolman at the center of the dilemma took an appointment with Doc Weaver, who confirmed Hambone's diagnosis, although he was prescribed a much more sensible treatment. The others, thusly afflicted or who considered themselves at risk, also lined up for professional help.

Having to cover a vast area of terrain daily, each patrolman kept a radio strapped to their waist, allowing them to communicate when a skier needed help or to coordinate avalanche duties. However, it soon became apparent that guidelines needed to be established to keep the airwaves professional, especially when patrolmen were often within earshot of skiers. "What you broadcast over the radio is often in a patient's face," Doug reminded them.

"Speak only when spoken to and follow the ABCs; that's Accuracy, Brevity, and Clarity," he said, counting them off his fingers. "And stop making up nicknames for each ridge, trail, and slope. They have official names, so use them. Greeley Pass is not Piss Pass and the Seven Sisters Pass is not the Seven Whores!"

It proved to be a challenging task, but Lynn and his buddies found ways around it. Since the language needed to be kept professional, they created codes to stand for what they wanted to say. They were all 800 numbers, with 821 meaning "Go pound sand up your ass," and another that meant, "Tell that to someone who gives a shit." Although there was a silver lining every time someone messed up, a tradition that spanned decades and may still be in use today. Each time a patrolman was caught using inappropriate language over the radio, they owed the rest of the patrol a case of beer, usually to be consumed at the end-of-day meeting in the patrol shack. In fact, any time a bad call or mistake was made, they owed a case of beer. It took years to clean up the radio talk and countless gallons of alcohol, but eventually, progress was made.

After a long day on the mountainside, the crew met back at the patrol shack for their post-shift meeting. Before plopping down on one of the couches, Lynn walked over to the soda machine and tossed in a quarter. However, soda was not what popped out of the bottom because this machine was stocked with beer. "There's nothing like ending a workday with twenty-five-cent beers," he said.

"Cheers!" the rest of the team agreed.

During Lynn's early years on the patrol, his next move would have been to drive himself home, but, when he made the cut into a full-time position, he got upgraded to a carpool with the rest of the guys who lived at the base of the canyon. Every night before leaving the resort, Lynn hopped into the back of the suburban, and the group pulled up to their favorite restaurant, the Shallow Shaft. It was famous for having waitresses who enjoyed flashing just about anyone who asked. The patrolmen gave a honk, and soon a handful of ladies walked up to a big window, pulled up their shirts, and slammed their breasts against the glass. Happily, Lynn and the group waved goodnight and pulled away, anxious for another day on the slopes.

Lynn had joined the patrol at the encouragement of a friend and fellow ski patrolman, Bentsen Moss. The two had been working together at Lynn's father's family business when Bentsen told Lynn the patrol needed a part-time man. The patrol did not host try-outs, so Bentsen sponsored Lynn and assured the boss, Doug Christenson, he was a capable skier. What Bentsen failed to mention was Lynn's age. Since Lynn didn't know there was a minimum age requirement and it didn't come up in the interview, he was hired. Three years later when Lynn turned twenty-one, the patrol threw him a big birthday party in commemoration of reaching the legal limit. Doug had been unaware of the age violation when he walked in on the lively comradery and saw the cake on the table.

"What's all the fuss about?" he asked.

"It's Lynn's twenty-first birthday!" they cheered.

"What?! You've been underage this whole time?!"

A few weeks later, Lynn and his buddies were enjoying their favorite hangout spot, the bar at the Gold Miner's Daughter lodge. Over the last several days, there had been enough snowfall for the resort to institute an Interlodge ban, restricting people from going outside or from driving up and down the canyon due to the high risk of avalanche danger. Before the all-clear could be given, the patrol would need to dispel any potential avalanches, but that would have to wait until first light the next morning. In the meantime, they intended to relax.

"It's another Interlodge ban, boys. You know what to do," Lynn grinned. They grabbed a set of white bedsheets from the hospitality closet and snuck outside into the frosty darkness. Shaking out the housekeeper's meticulous folding job, they threw the sheets over themselves and camouflaged into the snow. As they crept through the fresh powder, they followed the faint glow coming from the next lodge over. The objective of this covert operation was the same as the many that came before—bar hopping.

"Keep an eye out for Tripod," someone whispered.

"The three-legged coyote?" Lynn asked.

"Yeah, we're supposed to radio in any sightings," he said.

"You're just afraid of running into him in the dark," someone else added.

"Well, coyotes are nocturnal," Lynn added.

Once they reached the door to the Sitzmark Club lounge, Lynn kicked the snow from his boots, and they filed in. They each got a round of drinks when Hambone suddenly, and inexplicably, began taking his shirt off. Hambone was a man with a permanently furrowed brow and was considered a loose cannon. As a few new people walked in, he stood up and bellowed, "No tops allowed in this bar!" Lynn looked down at his drink to avoid any collateral attention, but when he peeked around the room, he noticed the customers didn't seem thrown by the new rule, and many began to comply. Perfect strangers took their shirts off, including women of varying ages who were now down to their bras. Lynn admired Hambone for his bold and unpredictable inspirations. The group stayed for a few more drinks until Lynn saw Hambone open a second-story window, climb out, and scale down the brick wall back into the snow.

One night, they held a party where everyone was overdoing themselves. Doug followed Hambone out to the parking lot where he watched the man walk on all fours and bite the car tires. "He had a few screws loose and there might have been a head injury in his past, but he was an excellent patrolman," Doug said.

Spontaneity ran deep among the patrolmen, demonstrated by their annual spring raffle which offered two plane tickets to a mystery destination. The patrolmen purchased the tickets for twenty to thirty dollars apiece and then went home and packed their suitcases. They all met up at the Salt Lake City airport, dressed and ready to go, and began drawing names out of a bowl. As each name was pulled, those tickets were eliminated until the last two remained. As the winners were announced, they collected their tickets and jumped on a plane, since in those days tickets were transferrable and passengers didn't need fourteen forms of ID. Everyone else returned home as the winners headed somewhere like Las Vegas, Florida, or the Caribbean.

3

Rescues

Each year on Christmas and New Year's Eve, Alta hosts a Night Run, a procession of thousands of skiers slowly zigzagging down the mountain on a single path while lighting up the sky with handheld torches. These trails of fire are a stark contrast against the dark mountain and look like a volcano spewing lava down its banks. After my parents were married and my sister, Alyssa, and I were three years old, our parents let us participate by tucking us between their legs and helping us hold our little skis in a permanent V-shape for speed control, a position often called "Pie" or "Pizza," for kids.

"Hold on tight, Buggy," my dad would say as he clutched my little mitts in his hands.

He shared his love of skiing with Alyssa and me the day we could fit into ski boots, but he didn't teach us how to ski himself because he had already tried to teach others and failed. Novice skiers on the slopes would ask for advice, and my dad would watch them ski a short distance and then topple into a ball.

Alta's Night Run
University of Utah Archives

"What did I do wrong?" they would ask.

"I have no idea," was the best answer he could give them.

Instead, he signed us up with one of the professional instructors and proudly watched from the sidelines as we inched around flags on the bunny hill, our arms outstretched in our puffy, winter coats like Ralphie in *A Christmas Story*.

I regret not skiing regularly as a teen and now have to re-learn each time I make it up to the slopes. On a ski trip with our church's youth program, I was asked by an older teen how long I had been skiing. I proudly answered, "Since I was three." My pride prevented me from being honest about my actual skills as a skier, and, when we arrived, the experienced teens welcomed me in as one of them, leading me into the lift line for a black diamond trail, the code word for skill-level expert. As we jumped off the lift and started down the mountainside, I was petrified to see a skinny path of ice sandwiched between a mountain wall and a cliff. I slid on my butt in a desperate attempt to not sail off the edge and into oblivion. When I finally reached a plateau of safety, I took a full sigh of relief, but I knew I had a long way to go before I would reach the base. My friend saw the obvious shortcoming in my abilities and helped me down the rest of the way. From then on, I kept to the trails best suited to my expertise, or lack thereof, and understood the importance of being honest.

....

While on patrol one afternoon, my dad picked up his radio and was called to the side of a pretty young woman who had injured her leg. As he knelt beside her and prepped the wooden splint, he asked her to fill out an information card with her name and address. As he adjusted the splint, he noticed she had written Palance as her last name, and the street address was Hollywood Blvd. Curious, he asked, "What do you do for a living?"

"I'm an actress."

"Any relation to Jack Palance?"

"Yeah, that's my dad."

Jack Palance was famous for playing scary characters in black and white movies and later the part of Curly Washburn, a man with skin so leathery he "looked like a saddlebag with eyes", in the 1991 movie *City Slickers* Lynn focused his attention back on the woman's injury, but he struggled to fit the splint to her leg and was jostling it around as they talked. The splint reached the entire length of her leg, but Lynn had been keeping his attention focused down by her shin and ankle.

"Quit jamming that thing in my crotch!" she said.

"Sorry!" Lynn hadn't been paying attention to what had been going on with the other end.

Lynn saw other celebrities, like John Wayne, from a distance as the reputation of Alta's world-renowned snow lured many members of the rich and famous. Most celebrities were assigned a ski patrolman to accompany them, and one day Lynn was assigned Robert Redford, who showed up wearing an effective disguise of grungy ski clothes with patches of duct tape. Lynn enjoyed making the runs with him, but halfway through the day he got a page on the radio.

"You need to take a call at the base," it said. Lynn excused himself and hurried off, leaving Redford to trudge over to the lift line and wait for his return. Just as Lynn high-tailed it back, Redford was boarding the lift, and the staff called out over the crowd for singles, meaning there was a chair with an empty spot. Lynn waved his arm and volunteered, jumping into the empty spot right behind Redford. The actor was sitting next to a young girl and, for the moment, everything was peaceful. Their chairs carried them over the treetops, and Lynn tried to brush the top branches with the tips of his skies. Suddenly, the girl let out a scream.

"Oh no," Lynn thought, knowing the girl must have just realized who she was sitting next to. When they disembarked, he asked Redford if that kind of fangirling bothered him. "No, I love that stuff," he said.

Then there was Richard Masur, a tall man from the movie *The Thing*. He and Lynn chatted during each trip up the lift, and then he later confessed to feeling ashamed for recently portraying a child molester in the film *Fallen Angel*.

To Lynn, the real stars were military brass. When the Secretary of Navy, John Lehman, came to ski on several occasions, Lynn was assigned as part of the man's "detail." Duties included having lunch with him, riding lifts, and, of course, skiing with the group. Lehman was fluent in five languages and flew jet airplanes in his leisure time. Lynn noticed an aide, called Spike, who didn't know how to ski but was somehow expected to keep up. On one lift trip, Lynn sat next to the cutest girl in the entourage.

"Is that your dad up ahead?" he asked, motioning to Secretary Lehman in the next chair.

"No, that's my husband."

"Oh!"

Then there were admirals like James E. Service, the man in charge of the entire Pacific fleet. While with him, Lynn boldly asked, "How much does it cost taxpayers to fly you from Coronado to Alta?"

"That's classified," he replied. Then continued, "Do you know Air Force F-16s?"

"Yeah."

"Those are about $20,000 an hour. Our Naval planes are way more expensive."

On another occasion, Senator Ed Kennedy flew in with an entourage whom he sent to the main office.

"We're here with Senator Kennedy," an aid announced, "and it's his first-time skiing at Alta. He'd like to try it out."

"Great!" the president of Alta replied with a genuine smile as he walked over to the window and pointed, saying, "There is where you buy your ticket, and that's where you get in line." They didn't stay and instead spent the day at Snowbird.

On the rare occasion a lift would break down, Lynn helped with the petrifying process of evacuating riders from chairs perched high in the treetops, and, invariably, some would be suspended over steep, treacherous cliffs. Knowing the process could take hours, the patrol divided into teams and began tossing ropes over the lift cables, using them to lift a little cart up to the butt of each chair. Lynn had to then coax the skier to leave the safety of the chair and crawl onto the tiny platform. When that feat was accomplished, which often felt impossible, Lynn and the team slowly lowered them down as they clung for dear life. "It was a spectacular sight," Lynn said. The patrol practiced these scenarios once every fall, but once while a patrolman was being self-evacuated, he grabbed the wrong rope and fell, breaking both legs. He was assigned the snowmobile for the rest of the winter.

One beautiful winter day, a family was enjoying the fresh snowfall when their ten-year-old daughter was injured on the slopes. As soon as Lynn got the call over the radio, he swept down the hillside to where her family was waiting, unclipped his boots from his skis, and knelt beside her.

"I'm here to help," he reassured her. "Let's get you off this mountain."

Her eyes were as wide as dinner plates, and the mild temperature of the air did not explain her intense shivering. He knew she was scared and tried to comfort her as he carefully braced her leg and lifted her onto the bright orange sled. As he strapped her in, he wrapped her in a water-proof blanket to shield her from the rushing cold air and snow spray that was sure to engulf her when they got moving. He snapped back into his skies and grabbed the two poles extending from the front of the toboggan. As he gently guided her sled to the base, her family remained alongside.

Years later, when I was born, he gave me her name, Brichelle, and I'm proud to carry her memory. I have never met anyone else with that name, although I know it's an old English name. While introducing myself, I am often asked to repeat it a couple of times and then spell it, which is why I usually go by my nickname, Shelly. Although, I often hesitate before giving my nickname because I don't want my parents to think I prefer it over the name they gave me, even if it's just because of the fuss. In fact, nothing could be farther from the truth. I adore my name and wouldn't have it any other way. And, as the cherry on top, my dad gave me his first name as my middle name, a Falkner family tradition of giving the father's first name to be the middle name for the child. When my first daughter was born, I carried on that tradition and gave her the middle name Brichelle.

4

Beef It Up

Nitro exhaust burns your eyes but smells so good. Rumbling at the starting line, Lynn revved his engine until it roared. This AAA class beast had a 3,000 horse-power engine at his back and was propelled by four gnarly rear paddle tires, the dirt version of a pedal boat wheel often found in ponds or resort beaches. With a five-inch diameter fuel line, Lynn's racer burned a gallon of fuel a second. He had started his racing career right out of high school, beefing-up Jeeps, but when enthusiasts started building sand dragsters, he knew he had to be a part of it. Now, in his mid-twenties, he switched out his gasoline-fed Jeep with a monster that consumed nitro, a substance so powerful it had to be diluted with alcohol.

Camper trailers dotted the flat, dry landscape while massive crowds swarmed the dirt strip. A deep rumble of engines could be heard for miles. A red CJ7 Jeep with a white hardtop sat amongst the mass of off-roaders. That was Lynn's toy, too, although it was more practical than the one he sat in at the moment.

Lynn and the "MEPCO Special"

Tires with traditional treads were rarely used in this soft, sandy terrain since paddle tires had an edge that couldn't be beaten. The first time Lynn used them, they were so powerful they spun right off the wheels. From then on, he had to screw the rubber to the metal to keep them in place. The combination of paddle tires and a powerful engine made these machines unstoppable on sand mountains. You couldn't even stack sand steep enough to slow them down, and the racers still flew right off the top. Organizers tried to make the competitions fair, like changing the air pressure to reduce traction to prevent the sport from turning into a drag race on a hill.

Lynn started with two rear tires but soon realized the power of his engine demanded that he double it. In contrast, the nose of the vehicle was fastened to two wheels that could rival a toddler's tricycle. The car measured over twenty feet long, weighed 1,300 pounds, and was custom-built to fit him. A group of contracted welders pieced together the frame while his family's Jeep parts company, MEPCO, put the engine in. To help promote the company, Lynn named the racer the "MEPCO Special."

As he strapped into the driver's seat, adrenaline coursed through him. His pit crew, made of a group of guys he worked alongside at the company, rolled him to the starting line. Among them was his young brother, Chris, a coat-tailing fan who loved having a big brother who raced. At school, Chris drew pictures of race cars with dirt flying up as they flew down the track. They made for great stories, telling his grade-school class about his brother's racecar being the fastest on the Salt Flats. He was the son of Lynn's mother, Colleen, and her second husband, Alvie Carter, a gentle man who shared her passion for art and a was popular performer at Kingsbury Hall when the production *Showboat* came to town. He sang "Ol' Man River" with as much soul as Paul Robeson in the original 1936 film, and it remained his favorite song to sing every Thanksgiving when our families got together. I'm not sure which he loved more, spending time with family or the chili powder in my mother's pumpkin pie.

Colleen and Alvie had married in 1970 after years of keeping their relationship a secret. Interracial marriages had become legal in Utah seven years prior, but social acceptance was still decades away. Alvie spent the majority of his life working as a laborer at Kennecott Copper Mine, a massive open-pit that dug into the side of the Oquirrh Mountains. His impressive ability to drive railroad spikes into the ground had made him akin to the folk tales of John Henry. When my sister and I were young, we often spent the day at his house, listening to him sing from their bedroom as we learned pottery and painted ceramics with our grandmother. He kept a smile in his eye and whistled beautiful bird songs to me when I was too shy to hold a conversation.

Back at the track, Lynn fixed his eyes onto the vertical light post in front of him, the "Christmas Tree," which would signal the start of the race. He watched as the top light lit up. Yellow.

Then the next two lights yellow, and another yellow. This was it. When the bulb at the bottom turned green, Lynn smashed his foot into the accelerator, and the tires spun into a fury. An explosion of sound hit the crowd, and Lynn and his competitor were off in a cloud of dust. A fan in the crowd snapped a picture that was almost a complete blur. "That's exactly what it feels like from inside one of those racers, a blur," Lynn said.

It was Bakersfield, California, and he had reached 143 mph within 100 yards. Lynn pumped his fist into the air with a shout when his time of 2.75 seconds was announced. He had broken the world record. However, there wasn't much time for celebrating because another racer topped his record just twenty minutes later. As Lynn looked behind him at the dust cloud-covered track, he could see Chris and the rest of the crew pile into the back of the team truck, speed over to pick him up, and haul the racer back.

"Can I ride in the racer again?" Chris pleaded.

"Sure thing, kid."

As Lynn climbed out of the cage, Chris hopped in with a smile that stretched from one side of his face to the other. The crew hooked the racer up to the truck and Lynn plopped his helmet onto Chris's head. Four feet tall on a good day, Chris felt ten feet tall sitting in that racer and riding past a crowd of onlookers as they pulled it back down the raceway and through the starting gate.

Lynn was introduced to racing through his father's company, MEPCO, short for Military Equipment and Parts Company. He had started tailing his father, Don, to work by the age of five, and, in 1959, the company was born from one hundred tons of surplus military Jeep parts purchased at an auction. With no storefront, the parts piled up in the family's yard where Lynn and his little brother, Mark, were tasked with finding useful pieces to sell. Their father sold it piece by piece, here and there, and everywhere. Eventually, Don fashioned a storefront out of a tiny building, a bunch of shelving, and a computer the size of a closet.

At the time, Jeeps were coming off the factory line with inherent flaws, so MEPCO's mission became finding and building solutions. They slowly became known as the Jeep experts, and MEPCO became the living example of the business motto, "Find a need and fill it." As Lynn reached his late teenage years, he nudged MEPCO into the racing world, and the company sponsored a Jeep called the Bronco Buster #44, a trash-talking message to the only other Jeep-like vehicle of the era, the Ford Bronco. Since MEPCO was a Jeep supply shop, they had more than a little Jeep team spirit going on. The first race was in Elko, Nevada, with Lynn tagging along behind the Bronco Buster's owner, who raced quite poorly. The man allowed Lynn to try it himself, and he won every subsequent heat he entered. Impressed by Lynn's success, the man relinquished the Jeep to him, saying, "It's yours."

Lynn bought an old M38-A1 army jeep, like the ones on the TV show, *M.A.S.H.*, and beefed it up with a Chevy V8 engine. In those days, the racecourses included an obstacle course, hill climb, and dirt drag race, each scored to the fastest time. Lynn raced every chance he got, promoting MEPCO at each event, traveling to Nevada, Wyoming, California, and the Salt Flats of the Great Salt Lake.

Lynn in his Jeep and paddle tires

Listening to my dad tell me of his off-road racing filled me with awe, but he solidified his love of Jeeps the day he drove a 1949 Willy's into our gravel driveway. I was sixteen, and that candy-red beauty became my whole world. I now wish to apologize for the damage I inflicted on its transmission as I learned how to drive a manual, but that Jeep, and my dad, taught me everything I know. It had more than its share of quirks, and I loved every one of them: useless windshield wipers I'm sure were pulled off a Barbie car, a maximum speed of forty-five miles per hour (downhill), and side mirrors that rattled to an extent that using their reflections was pointless. It was built before turn signals, so I had to stick my arm out the window and make gestures like a bicyclist. The steering wheel reminded me of a school bus, and, without power steering, I had to throw my body into it to make each curve. Oh, how I loved that Jeep.

The engine broke down frequently, like the one time on a dark and open stretch of backroad at 5:30 in the morning on my way to band practice. As I stood on the cold asphalt and stared into the blackness overlooking the valley, I could only make out the faint glow on the horizon and the cattle fencing that lined the road. With repeated failed attempts to get my parents on the phone, I contemplated my options. I knew I could hike the seven miles to school, carrying my trombone case, or walk the two miles home.

I began my return trip down the eerily quiet road when a pair of headlights appeared. A lump rose to my throat as I realized the headlights gave the driver a clear view of me while blinding my ability to see them. I didn't know whether to act like I needed a ride, risk getting in a car with a psycho, or pretend, I was walking along the dark pastureland on purpose with a broken-down vehicle right behind me. I shielded my eyes as the car pulled up, but felt a sense of relief when I peered inside and saw an elderly lady. She said she was on her way to work and was happy to give me a ride to school. I gladly accepted. Thankfully, this story had a happy ending, and my body wasn't buried in the nearby canyon.

A few days later, I left school and drove through the surrounding neighborhood, stopping at the stop signs that seemed to spring from every corner. Suddenly, I felt the brake pedal lose its resistance, and, within moments, the pedal became entirely unresponsive. I pulled the emergency brake, but the Jeep continued to roll down the street, albeit slower. I managed to get the Jeep down to a crawl but saw another stop sign approaching, and I knew the Jeep was about to roll through it.

Attempting to protect my hot-off-the-press driver's license, I leaped from the driver's seat and into the road, an easy move since I had left my fabric "doors" at home. I ran in front of the vehicle to stop it myself, a move I knew was risky even at a crawl.

The Jeep had a high clearance, and I figured it might "clear" me if I ended up underneath it. I just needed to steer clear of the tires. Using my body weight, I threw myself into the grill and pushed as hard as I could, trying not to get bowled over as it pushed me backward. I finally got it to a stop inches from the next sign, and I breathed a sigh of relief knowing my license was safe for another day. As usual, my dad came to the rescue, and, before I knew it, I was back on the road blasting tunes from my wind-up radio buckled into the passenger seat.

That Jeep was always up for whatever we could throw at it. We painted the red cross on it, removed the windshield, and drove it to the neighborhood drive-in movie theater when we entered the annual Trunk O' Treat contest dressed as the cast from *M.A.S.H.* Of course, in preparation for the event, we properly raided the Army Surplus Store, but we didn't realize the *M.A.S.H.* theme song we played during the parade included the lyrics, which kept repeating "Suicide is painless" to the neighborhood kids.

Whenever there was a good snowfall, we used the Jeep to pull sleds and inflatable tire tubes through the pasture. We would ramp up momentum and then pull it into tight donuts, drifting like a *Fast and Furious* movie as we hurtled the sled around until the rider could no longer hang on and flew off into the snow. I'm not sure which was more exciting, being on the sled or in the Jeep because screaming took place in both locations. Usually sitting in the passenger seat was my cousin, Ian, and we clung for dear life as the world blurred around us, and we laughed until we cried. The pasture wasn't as safe as it seemed with sharp irrigation heads poking from the ground where we hooked up pipelines during the summer. If an irrigation head was hit at high speed, which was the only speed we knew how to go, it would have shredded the tire tube and done untold damage to whoever was riding it. Thankfully, no one was ever hurt, but there was an incalculable number of close calls, including the time I accidentally sent my neighbor, Austin Jasper, right into one, and, by some miracle, he sailed over the top.

We attempted the sledding with our Ford F-350 truck, but it got stuck the moment it left the driveway. As it sat there in the middle of the open gate, it looked defeated having failed the first test of off-road sporting. We retrieved the Willy's Jeep, which was a fraction of the truck's size and weight, and used it to pull the truck back onto the driveway with ease. We put the tubes back on the Jeep and finished another day of screaming while being force-fed snow mixed with a bit of car exhaust.

My sister proved to be her father's daughter the day she pulled a nifty stunt in the high school parking lot. She and I pulled in early that morning for six o'clock jazz band practice, Alyssa in the Ford truck, and me in the Willy's. At such an early hour, the parking lot was still empty except for a couple of other band nerds, but the previous night's snowplow had used the leftovers from the latest blizzard to build a mountain of snow in the middle. She must have been thinking of the nifty poses Jeeps often strike in dealerships and on social media posts because she drove that truck straight up the snowbank and perched the front tires at the top. The angle was so steep, her rear tires were still on asphalt, but she must have thought if a Jeep could do it, then so can a truck. She left it there all day, and I was so proud.

As my dad raced his beloved Jeeps, he soon realized the sport was beginning to change, and he knew he needed to adapt with it. Vehicles were now being designed for specific courses, so he transitioned from the boxy Jeep to the long, skinny body of a sand drag car nicknamed sand rails. However, his first run was a far cry from the epic debut he imagined. As Lynn went tearing down the track with screaming engines and plumes of dust, he was racing faster than he ever had before. Closing in on the finish line, he readied his finger on the button that would deploy both the brakes and the parachute. In drag racing, much like skydiving, when it's time to hit the brakes, a small parachute is deployed and it uses the power of the wind to pull out a large parachute. Without these chutes, racecars would take an enormous amount of track to slow down.

As Lynn crossed the finish line to a cheering crowd, he hit the brakes and punched the button for the parachutes. Out popped the mini parachute, but he had forgotten to tie it to the larger chute, so it flew out the back and fizzled through the air before settling, unceremoniously, onto the track. Without the main parachute, Lynn took an exceptionally long stretch of track before finally coming to a stop. His pit crew refused to get caught in the embarrassment and insisted he make the "walk of shame" himself. As Lynn passed the watching crowd, he scooped up the baby parachute and made the long walk back.

As the "car guy" on the ski patrol, other patrolmen were using Lynn frequently to get parts and help them with their vehicles. He helped Court Richards change out the clutch plate in his Bronco and helped Doug trick out his '72 Chevy Blazer. The Blazer was looking good when they finished with it, so Lynn asked to borrow it for a car show, explaining that he would polish it up nice and make that chrome glisten. Doug agreed, and the vehicle took first place in the competition. However, when the Blazer was returned, Doug realized Lynn had only polished the side of the vehicle that was presented. The car was only half done.

In hopes of helping run MEPCO for the long run, Lynn signed up for a semester of business classes at the University of Utah. As he pulled into the parking lot on the first day of class, he stepped out with books in hand, anticipating a good start to the semester. However, he couldn't stop staring at the beautiful, snow-covered mountains, and glanced at the roof of his car where his skis were strapped. "I'll make it up tomorrow," he said and jumped back in to head for the slopes. Each morning played out the same, he would pull into campus only to look at the mountains and talk himself into believing his absences could be made up later. His second semester was no different, and he ended his first year of college with a 0.0 GPA. When he decided to return to college years later, he would have to beg the University for forgiveness.

5

Marooned

They had been stranded on the island for six weeks. When it had been time to leave three weeks ago, the seaplane pilot never showed up. Lynn's group radioed in on Tuesday morning, as instructed, but all they heard was silence. They called Tuesday night, Wednesday morning, and Wednesday night. After several weeks, someone finally answered their hail and reported the pilot had gone back to the mainland. They were stranded. The Australian caretaker in the group spoke up, "The island we need to get to is Magero, and it's in that direction," he said, motioning across the vast Pacific. "No one is coming to rescue us, so, if you want to get out of here, we can take the boat and head in that direction. Of course, if we miss, we'll be floating until we reach Japan someplace, as the currents go."

Lynn had been invited on this trip as a plus one with his mother. It was a generous offer to go scuba diving in the Marshall Islands by an acquaintance who had been trying to create a diver's paradise for the rich and famous, a place where few feet had touched. The endeavor didn't pan out, but he planned one last hurrah before returning the lease for the island. It would be three weeks of diving in crystal blue waters, so Colleen and Lynn were happy to accept. Colleen knew the entrepreneur from the tropical fish he supplied to her antique shop, including a pet octopus, which was not for sale. The octopus was shy around unfamiliar people, usually hiding in the rocks, but it became curious when it recognized someone. Whenever Lynn put his hand on top of the water, it would send a tentacle up, wrap around his wrist, and pull him down to where its house was.

Lynn, still in his early twenties, and his mother flew with a group of nine other divers from Salt Lake City to the middle of the South Pacific. Their first stop was Hawaii, and then crow-hopped to a place called Johnson Island, a military zone charged with disposing of weapons of mass destruction. Its descendant became the army depot in my hometown where my dad would later raise my sister and me. While growing up, we would occasionally hear a "Boom!" from across the valley, and moments later feel the floor shake and watch the blinds rattle against the windowpanes. I would run to the west side of the house to see a small plume of smoke lifting skyward against the base of the mountain. I loved those moments.

Our small farming community had sirens, much like the tornado warnings of the Midwest. The difference was that we don't have tornadoes in Utah or anything else that usually requires a warning system. We had sirens to prepare us for potential leaks from one of the three military bases surrounding our valley, each dealing with a variety of dangerous substances, and most of which were classified. Wednesday afternoons were marked by a blaring serenade of "THIS IS A TEST," followed by dogs howling to the rising and falling of the siren.

As the dive group came in over Johnson Island, Lynn noticed the landing strip was built on a peninsula so narrow the ocean could be seen on both sides of the plane. Once on the tarmac, he and the other passengers were prohibited from getting out, and, instead, a crew came and unloaded the plane's food and supplies for the locals. The aircraft carried mainly cargo since not many people traveled to the area. Its schedule went from east to west one week and back the next, so the only time someone could catch a ride was when it was already going in the right direction.

Once the cargo was unloaded, they returned to the skies. The next stop was a central hub in the Marshall Islands before the last leg to a secluded location within the region. As they neared the area, the pilot announced over his radio a list of prohibited items that could not be taken into the Islands. Since it was their next stop, Lynn thought the announcement seemed too little, too late.

"The number one restricted item that can NOT be brought in is a firearm."

"Oops," Lynn thought, keeping the knowledge of his illicit item to himself as he considered what to do with it.

When they landed at the small regional airport, a man jumped on board and introduced himself as their next pilot. He then herded everyone to a nearby shoreline, where he presented his 1941 PBY, its belly submerged and rocking in the waves like the breast of a duck. Lynn was still mulling over what to do with the illegal contraband in his bag when he decided to sneak over to a vacant beach to dispose of it. As he reached the opposite shoreline, he glanced around to check that the coast was clear, and then chucked his .357 revolver into the ocean.

He slogged back through the sand to the PBY where the pilot noticed Lynn gazing at its toweringly high wings.

"These wings double as the plane's fuel tank," the man said proudly. "And it's amphibious. The pontoon floats hanging from the wings have small wheels underneath, along with retractable landing gear on the belly, that allows me to set it down on both land and sea." Lynn thought back to his high school history class and a few action-filled war movies and remembered these planes had been used heavily during WWII. He noticed the rest of the group was loading their gear, so Lynn grabbed his bag and followed the jetty up to the plane. The pilot helped him climb inside and handed him his bag. Lynn crept down the aisle and checked on his mother to make sure she was comfortable and had what she needed. Then, turning around, he headed up front to satisfy some curiosity. He stuck his head into the cockpit and admired the numerous switches and controls.

"Do you need a co-pilot?" Lynn asked.

"Yes!" the pilot welcomed, not realizing the question had been a joke. Lynn hopped into the seat next to him and peered at all the gauges. Noticing a pair of binoculars on the dash, he tried looking through them, but they were completely pacified. He saw a tag attached and flipped it over, noticing the binoculars were also from 1941. "They must be just for show," Lynn thought. He watched the pilot flip some switches and bring the engine to life. As they took off from the ocean and into the skies like a regular sea bird, it was humbling to see the vast expanse of

STEEP TERRAIN

ocean reaching from one horizon to the other. For most of the trip, land couldn't be found at all.

Lynn noticed one of the passengers was an older fellow, and listened as he told the other passengers he had fought in this area during WWII. As the plane neared the remote island, Lynn watched him become uneasy. The man said he was nervous about the possibility of finding Japanese soldiers since "holdouts" had been seen on Pacific islands as late as 1974. The Japanese Bushido code, or "way of the warrior," forbade the notion of surrender and, after the war had ended, many of these soldiers were found often attacking intruders because they either didn't believe Japan had surrendered or because the fighting had severed communications, and they were unaware the war had ended.

Approaching the diving destination, the pilot called to Lynn over the roar of the engines, saying, "Okay, give me ten-degree flaps!"

"What are flaps?" Lynn called back. The truth was revealed.

"Take this and screw it down until the needle comes to ten."

Lynn started cranking the flaps manually and, as the plane descended, he saw the ocean heaving with big ocean swells. "I sure hope that's not our landing zone," he thought. Thankfully, the pilot steered around to an atoll where smooth, peaceful waters were protected by an arc of several small islands. A beautiful lagoon came into view, which looked as if it had been painted by a master of seascapes. As they landed and taxied up to the shore, Lynn gazed at the blue waves, each sparkling at the crest. The sand shimmered in the sun's rays, and the scene looked as if it had been pulled from the movie *Blue Lagoon*. Lynn became captivated by the serenity of this untouched paradise.

The PBY

Lynn followed the rest of the group as they jumped from the plane into the shallows of the shoreline, and then helped his mother exit the cabin and make her way onto the sand. He looked around and noticed the island had been outfitted with a building for gasoline as well as oxygen for their scuba tanks. Before departing and returning to the main island, the pilot handed the group a radio and said, "I'll be back in three weeks. If you get into trouble, call any Tuesday at 9 am." With an emergency plan like that, Lynn hoped they wouldn't need to use it.

Lynn walked up the pearly white beach and saw tents had been set up for them, and he and his mother were each given their own. He took a walk to explore the island, and, as the sun dipped, he was amazed at how far the water receded with the tide. It must have been twenty feet or more. He could see forever, and the tide pools left behind were plump full of crabs and various other creatures. He also saw eels traveling through the coral from one tide pool to the next, eating trapped fish like they were at a buffet table.

In the middle of the island, he found a well with fresh drinking water, but made the mistake of tossing the bucket down the hole without securing the other end of the rope. Embarrassed at the thought of having to ask for help, Lynn attempted to retrieve the bucket himself. He scaled the slippery, moss-covered walls and clawed at the rock crevasses to make the fifteen-foot drop to the bottom. "It would be even more embarrassing if they find me dead down here," he thought. As he reached the bottom, he grabbed the bucket and, thankfully, climbed back up without incident.

Swimming in Micronesia was like nothing he had ever experienced. The warm, crystal-clear waters and the explosion of tropical sea life were a stark contrast to Lynn's first diving experience. His uncle George had taken him to Blue Lake, the ironically named oasis of murky, green wetlands on Utah's western border. Cattails and sagebrush lined the mossy shores of a flat landscape that stretched far enough to reveal the curvature of the earth. To keep the cluster of small lakes interesting for divers, the remains of several boats were placed on the bottom, including a metal sculpture of a hammerhead shark. The pools are fed by deep natural springs and bubbles that rise naturally from the sandy bed like a slow simmer in a kitchen saucepan. On a crisp winter day, Lynn would watch the steam rising off the rippling surface of these warm geothermal hot spots.

To scuba dive in the United States, divers must go through scuba certification, which is the diving equivalent of a driver's license. Breathing underwater, and therefore under pressure, requires knowledge of nitrogen buildup in the body, an essential ability to avoid potentially lethal complications like "the bends."

Lynn began training for his certification alongside one of his ski patrol buddies, a man named Hook. When it was time to breathe underwater for the first time, the two climbed into the bathwater-warm training pool at Neptune Divers in Salt Lake City and slunk under the surface. Lynn made a conscious effort to breathe through the regulator hose, an unnatural feeling that got significantly worse when he was asked to pull his mask off. As the water rushed over his eyes and nose, the instinct to hold his breath became almost impossible to ignore.

The instructor had been going from one set of diving partners to the next, giving them the thumbs up to ask if they were doing okay, but when the man reached Hook, there was a problem. Hook regularly kept his receding hairline covered with a toupee, but here under the water, it had begun to lift off his head and float away. Not knowing what to do, Hook had grabbed the mass and shoved it down the front of his swimming trunks. Lynn had previously been the only bald guy in the class, but now the instructor was looking at two.

"Who are you?" the instructor gestured.

"Oh!" was the reply on Hook's face as he reached into his pants and pulled out the hairy monster. Completely startled, the instructor rushed to the surface in a frenzy. Had they been in deep water, he would have been in serious trouble, but luckily, the man had a mere three feet to go before reaching the surface where he could regain his bearings.

While Alyssa and I were young, we would swim in the city pool with fins and snorkel masks, excited for the day we would be allowed to scuba dive too. When we reached the minimum age of ten, our dad signed us up, and we learned in the same training pool and under the same mentors as he did. When I turned fourteen, my first job was working at SeaBase, the natural saltwater spring on the other side of our hometown where divers can swim with an array of ocean life while still in the middle of the desert. It was owned by our scuba mentors, and the best part was feeding their three eight-foot nurse sharks.

I got to swim with the sharks during my certification and, on my days off, usually found them lazily dozing at the bottom. The water was relatively murky and had limited visibility, so I wouldn't see the sharks as I cruised along until they suddenly appeared in front of my face. They often let me pet them, and I loved the feeling of the fine-grade sandpaper texture of their skin. The rules were not to pet their tails or touch their face. Nurse sharks eat by sucking prey into their mouth like a vacuum, and even, though they don't have long teeth, a swimmer's hand would surely get bloodied up by being pulled back out. It happened to a visitor who stuck her hand in a dark cave without thinking about what might be lying inside.

On Lynn's first night in the Marshall Islands, he was preparing for sleep when a mysterious lump appeared under the bottom of his tent. He could hear scratching as it shifted around and dug through the sand. Too spooked to go outside and see what it was, Lynn tried stepping on it and beating it up a bit to scare it away. It eventually left, and Lynn was able to get some sleep, but he continued to wonder what that creature had been until a few days later when he saw a prehistoric-looking creature climbing a coconut tree.

Its pinchers were massive, and, as it reached the top, it snipped the stem of a coconut, sending it crashing to the ground.

Lynn felt the ground shake, and he knew he'd be in trouble if he ever got hit on the head by one. He watched another one of the creatures crack a coconut open with ease. He realized they were coconut crabs with their three-foot leg span and nine pounds of fightin' weight. As imposing as they were, Lynn was glad there weren't any harmful animal species on the island like snakes or anything else. The only troublesome pests were the flies. The island definitely had flies.

The diving was spectacular. Giant clams underwater during high tide would be left exposed as the tide left. With gaping mouths open to the air, they now sought food from the skies. Lynn enjoyed seeing sharks on many of his dives, usually blacktip reef sharks, and appreciated that these five-foot, torpedo-shaped predators kept a safe distance from him.

A man from Australia, along with his wife and five-year-old daughter, stayed on the island as the group's caretaker. While Lynn was thirty-five feet deep enjoying another scuba dive, he felt a tap on his shoulder. Turning around, he saw the five-year-old girl, completely naked and waving excitedly. She mouthed the word "Hi!" before picking a large conch shell off the sandy bottom and heaving it to the surface, whipping her little feet behind her.

While relaxing in the sand one afternoon, Lynn overheard a call come in over the radio. "Have any of you seen a trimaran recently?" This sailing yacht was much like a catamaran, except it had three floats instead of two.

"There's been a report of one missing. We don't have the means to go looking for it, but thought we might as well check with you to see if you had seen one."

"No, sorry, we haven't," the group reported back.

Lynn was loving this exotic, island-living adventure. He had all the seafood and bananas he could eat, plus four Marshallese boys had been hired to help with whatever the group needed, including scaling the trees for fresh coconuts or plucking a lobster from a tidepool. Lynn watched the boys with fascination as they climbed coconut trees just as well as the wildlife. Lynn enjoyed pulling massive lobsters from the tide pools, and his favorite Marshallese helper would carry them back to the beach and cook them for him. When Lynn returned from the shoreline, he stretched out in the sand next to the small fire and watched the sun dip below the horizon. It only took a few minutes for his latest catch to turn bright red, and the boy yanked it from the boiling water and carefully handed him the steaming crustacean.

Cracking open the shell, Lynn pulled the juicy, white meat from the claws and plopped it in his mouth. It tasted as if it had already been smothered in butter, a luxury typical of lobsters pulled right from the ocean. It had a savory saltiness while also carrying a slight mineral sweetness, similar to a drop of honey in a spoon of water. It was usually dark when they ate dinner, which gave Lynn the suspicious feeling he was eating a lot of flies too.

Unexpectedly, when their three weeks had passed and it was time to leave, the pilot never showed up. The group called repeatedly, day after day, but when they were finally told the pilot had gone back to the mainland, they knew they would need to find their own way home. The island provided the basic necessities of freshwater, unlimited coconuts, and seafood, so Lynn was not worried about the situation. If Colleen had any misgivings, she didn't mention them either. Lynn had brought half a dozen books for the trip and read them several times while nestled in the shade of the trees.

Calling for help on the radio.
Micronesia

When the Australian caretaker stepped up and suggested they head for the island of Magero, there wasn't much discussion needed. The group piled into a small boat and left the safety of the island, soon heaving in the swells of the sea now that they had left the atoll. Before long, one of their motors burned up, so the Australian pulled it off and threw it into the ocean. They hoped the last motor would get them the rest of the way, but the situation became more doubtful. Without being sure of their direction, they also noticed the gas tank was running low. Thankfully, an island appeared on the horizon, and Lynn and the rest of the boat sighed with relief. They hit their target right on the mark.

Back in the regional hub, the island had many welcomed amenities. Lynn was especially excited about the movie theater and went with a few of the other young men to see the new Godzilla movie. Walking through the lobby, they came to a set of curtains leading into a dark theater room. As they passed through, the first guy fell with a "poof, poof, poof." Then the second guy, "Poof, poof, poof." Finally, the staff jumped up, warning them about the hidden step and preventing more of the guys from taking a tumble.

When they took their seats and the film began, Lynn and the others couldn't tell what language it was in. Someone said it was Japanese, but someone else said it was English with lousy sound. A scene came on where a boy and girl were kissing, and Lynn could hear bubble gum smacking loudly in the theater. The audience was full of kids who were uncomfortable with the intimacy and chewed extra loud to mask the awkward stillness. Lynn thought the movie looked exciting, but, without being able to understand the dialogue, he and the guys decided to try something else.

They checked into a motel and walked up to their room on the second floor. "Oh neat, a balcony!" Lynn said, opening the door and two windows. As he stepped onto the terrace, a chunk of rotten wood gave way, and he fell right through. In a split second, he caught the edge of the floor with his arms, saving himself from falling into the first floor. His buddies jumped to his aid and pulled him out and back into the room.

While out exploring the town, Lynn learned that anyone could be a taxi driver as long as they stuck a light to the roof of their vehicle. Taxis were cheap but required passengers to allow strangers to ride with them. When it was time to fly home and Lynn was on his way to the airport, his driver picked up two ladies, and they squeezed into the backseat with him. They spoke something to the driver in the local Ebon language. Lynn quickly discovered they had requested to go shopping, which meant they would be making several detours on the way, stopping at various shops and waiting for them to peruse for a while before piling back in and heading to the next one.

When Lynn reached the airport, he saw the rest of the divers from his group. The older gentleman who had previously been worried about "Japanese holdouts," had brought a young woman on the trip, whom he was dating. She was considerably younger than he was, and their age gap made them look quite out of place. Even though she was from Salt Lake City like the rest of the divers, her boyfriend was the manager of a small airport they would be passing through in Hawaii. When everyone landed back on the American islands for a plane changeover, Colleen traded her flight ticket with the young woman so Lynn could stay a few extra days. During this time, the young woman broke her relations off with the gentleman and began dating Lynn. The newly formed couple took great care to avoid the airport where her until-recently-ex-boyfriend was working. Despite the excitement, the relationship only lasted the length of the trip, and, once Lynn was home, life was back to normal.

6

Tragic Accident

When Lynn regained consciousness, he was in the middle of the freeway with his leg up by his ear. Everything was dark except the glow of the streetlights and the red and yellow beams coming off the cars passing by. "Where was the horse?" he thought.

When Lynn was fifteen years old, his stepmother, Lucy, kept a horse out behind the house. Ignoring his lack of experience, he decided to show off and go for a ride. However, once Lynn was on its back, the horse quickly tossed him and began galloping down the street. Lynn chased it through the neighborhood as it ran down each side street and over the neighbor's lawns. "Lucy is going to kill me!" he thought. Panicked, he watched the horse find its way onto the on-ramp to I-15, one of the busiest and fastest-moving roads in the state. Lynn carefully crossed the freeway, avoiding any oncoming cars, and caught up to the horse. He jumped back on, and both he and the horse returned to the highway, dreading to cross it again.

The evening had been wearing on, and as the sun began to fade, so was the traffic. Nonetheless, Lynn hopped off the horse and held the reins, just to be safe. He waited until no cars could be seen before beginning to lead the horse across. Suddenly, two cars appeared, and he could see the vehicles racing toward him. Lynn and the horse had just reached the middle lane, and he knew conflict was inevitable. Thankfully, the cars swerved and missed both of them, but a third car had been tailing behind the other two and hadn't seen them. As the car hit Lynn, he felt himself enter an out-of-body experience, looking down from above and watching the collision unfold. The vehicle's bumper hit his left leg, breaking his femur in two locations, and throwing him across the road. As he slammed into the asphalt, he received a skull fracture and scalping that would leave heavy scarring for the rest of his life.

When Lynn began to regain consciousness, a passerby pulled over to help and out jumped an Air Force medic. As he ran to Lynn's side, the medic began to pull Lynn's leg straight, sending a tidal wave of pain through his body. The man pressed down on the wound to slow the bleeding, and Lynn felt a slight sense of relief as the agony was momentarily eased. However, when the man let go, the sharp edges of bone ground against each other, and the torment returned with a vengeance. Unsure of how much time had passed, Lynn heard a siren blare an anthem as an ambulance arrived on the scene. With blinding lights flashing around them in the dark, Lynn felt he was on a movie set. The ambulance crew carefully but swiftly lifted him from the road and propped him into the back of the vehicle. It was a volunteer ambulance, and the crew struggled to drive through the ever-growing mass of slow-moving cars and rubbernecking drivers. One of the first responders opened the back door and yelled, "Get out of the way; this is an ambulance! We've got a critically injured person here!"

Lynn didn't know what happened to the horse during the collision, but somehow it was returned home unharmed. Lynn, on the other hand, was taken to Saint Mark's hospital where a crew of doctors and nurses attempted to put him back together. His mother was the first to arrive, completely distraught at his condition, and watched as he groaned in pain.

"Can't you sedate him or give him more pain medicine?" she asked one of the doctors.

"We're worried that with his head injury, the medication could put him in more danger."

Colleen sat at his bedside with tears streaming down her cheeks. Her mother, Leone, arrived and wrapped her in a hug, whispering, "Don't worry, he won't remember any of this." Mercifully, he never did. As the nurses prepped Lynn for surgery, his stepfather, Alvie, followed them into the hall and watched as they swept him away. When the surgery was complete and he began to wake up, his uncle Bruce came to visit, who noticed Lynn's gentle smile and how he didn't complain.

During the operation, a team of surgeons installed a metal shaft down his femur from his rear end to just above his knee. A set of bolts protruded from the skin along the side of his thigh where they helped stabilize the fractures, but they relentlessly rubbed through his flesh whenever he sat down. To this day, a prominent scar remains along his leg where the surgeons cut him open, and he has a slight limp because the bone didn't finish growing properly, leaving his left leg slightly shorter than his right. Lynn's hospital stay lasted five days, but the metal shaft had to remain an entire year, leaving him on crutches for nine months of high school.

When Lynn was born, Colleen was seventeen and his father, Don, was just a few years older. They were unable to afford a place of their own, so Colleen's parents offered the shed in their backyard, and the newlyweds made the most of it. Colleen's father, Marlow Fisher, was a pharmacist who ran a chemical supply business for local funeral homes, and the shed was his supply house. The stinging scent of formaldehyde clung to the air inside, and it rightfully earned the nickname "The Lab."

It wasn't long before a second child was born, Lynn's sister Ann, and they were often tended to by Colleen's little sister, Sylvia. During this time, Lynn's parents took a three-day trip, and his grandparents surprised them by fixing up "The Lab" into something a little more hospitable and family-friendly. Although the cabinets were still full of heavy chemicals and gallons of embalming fluid, they now had doors. It was an appreciated change, but after a few years, Don and Colleen were able to move into a home of their own across town.

Before the transition, Lynn's uncle Bruce often heard a knock at the back door only to find Lynn had arrived just in time for Saturday morning pancakes. While still a toddler, he would hold Bruce's hand as they took strolls through the local theme park, Lagoon, and girls would swoon at his long eyelashes and heavily freckled cheeks. Years later, the two spent summer days shooting BB guns, hunting big game in the forest, and hauling leaves to the burn pile.

When it came to trouble, Lynn had been taught by the best. Living with his uncles, who were three to five years older, there was no shortage of good ideas. It started with Lynn and George scraping sap off the trees in the backyard and melting it in a pan at their Aunt Jenny's house when no one was home. Then they painted the sap all over the furniture and walls before high-tailing it out of there before Jenny returned. Next were the pipe bombs made from the chemicals in Marlow's lab, and the reason George only has two fingers on his right hand, including his thumb. George had been only eight years old at the time of the accident and spent a good while in the hospital, both for the loss of his fingers and the burns to his face. "Oh, the things we did that could have cost our lives," Lynn recalled. "Even riding in a car under the back window curled up like a cat. Oh, it was heaven to ride in the car like that."

One day, George came to stay with Lynn at his home on Orchard Drive. George was ten years old at the time, but, when he noticed there were no adults around, he was promoted to the most senior on-premise. It was getting on toward supper, but there was no peanut butter or bread to be found—neither milk nor cereal. Six-year-old Lynn grabbed a bag of potatoes and pulled a chair up to the sink. He peeled a bowl full and tossed the potatoes into a frying pan, turning them into the best hash browns George had ever tasted. George later asked his mother, Leone, to cook potatoes like Lynn. They were good, but not like Lynn's.

At the ripe age of ten, Lynn and his neighborhood friend, Kevin Roberts, accidentally set fire to the forest that backed up to the family's property, unwittingly letting their campfire escape the confines of the pit. Thankfully, a group of neighbors came to the rescue and extinguished the flames before they proceeded past the tree line. Lynn and Kevin also decided to build a hideout, marching into the neighbor's field and digging a hole worthy of a hibernating bear. At eight feet long and eight feet wide, it was a mammoth-sized dugout, and they covered it with plywood boards and dirt for camouflage. Since it wasn't tall enough to stand in, they had to hunch over as they moved about. They carved shelves into the wall and proudly displayed their treasured knick-knacks. As the weeds began to grow over the dirt-covered roof, it was given enough camouflage to conceal it from the property owner and his backhoe. They didn't know it yet, but Lynn and Kevin's dugout was about to land them in big trouble.

7

Trouble

"Kevin!" Lynn called with excitement. "I think the neighbor's firing up his tractor!"

"Sweet!"

They ran to the back window of Lynn's house and peered out. They heard the engine growing louder and saw it appear around the corner, rumbling as it crawled across the lawn. However, when it turned and began heading out to the field, the boys' faces fell.

"Oh no. What if he drives over our dugout? He'll fall in!" Kevin said.

"No way. He'll see it. I'm sure he will," Lynn reassured him, but there was a crack in his voice.

Their eyes bulged as the backhoe headed straight for it.

"No!" the boys moaned. They scrunched their eyes to save themselves from the inevitable scene but couldn't help from peeking.

"We're going to be in so much trouble!" Lynn said, right before the backhoe plowed into the dugout, falling straight into the hole. Lynn and Kevin were stunned. They knew there would be serious consequences, but continued to watch as their shocked neighbor took a moment to realize his unexpected situation. Luckily for everyone involved, the machinery was built to maneuver similar situations, albeit not as extreme. He began alternating the hydraulic lifts on the front and back, slowly crawling out like a robot, one slow crank at a time. When the man was able to return his tractor and find both sets of their parents, Kevin and Lynn knew it was their hour of judgment.

"Kevin, you've got two choices," his mother said. "I can spank you right here on the lawn, or you can go to your room for the rest of the day."

He hung his head in defeat. "Spankings."

Kevin waited as his mother retrieved a hairbrush and pulled a chair down from their front porch.

"I'm ready," his mother said. Kevin shuffled over and slowly bent over her knee.

"Whap!" The hairbrush smacked him right over his jean pockets, and Lynn saw him wince.

"Whap!"

"Ow!" he yelped. After several more whacks, his mother set him free, and Lynn knew it was his turn.

"Lynn," Colleen said, gesturing for him to come close. "You know I don't like disciplining," she whispered, "but the whole neighborhood is watching, so you know I have to spank you too. I'm going to do it gently, so I need you to pretend it hurts, okay?"

"Okay," Lynn said in relief.

Colleen returned with a hairbrush of her own, and, as she bent him over her knee, she gave an exaggerated but gentle smack. Lynn faked a slight grimace.

"More," she whispered. "Act like it hurts." She pretended to hit him again.

"Ahh."

"Louder."

"Ahh!"

When the "spanking" was over, Colleen walked back inside, and Lynn and Kevin were free men once more.

Over the next few years, three more siblings were born, Lynn's little brothers Mark and Dane, followed by a second sister, Misty. Mark was the only child to break the brunette streak, sporting hair as red as fire, and inheriting even more freckles than Lynn. While propped up in his highchair one night, Mark begged Lynn for a piece of the chocolate cake that sat on their mother's kitchen counter.

"Please, please, please! Please!"

"No."

"PLEASE!!"

"No."

"PLEASE! PLEASE!"

"Fine!" Begrudgingly, Lynn carved off a slice from him but hesitated before returning. I can't blame my dad for what happened next. I suppose most siblings crack at one point, and most of us certainly fantasize about it. I once wished my parents would sell my sister to the zoo because she drove me bat crap crazy. Instead of immediately returning with the cake, Lynn cut the top off and filled the middle with Tabasco sauce. He then plopped the top back on and served it up to the salivating, wide-eyed toddler. Needless to say, Mark's happy grin turned to tears pretty quickly. Lynn regrets it to this day, citing it as a cruel offense against his brother.

When Mark turned five, the boy took an opportunity to relieve Lynn of his life savings. This consisted of three dollars worth of pennies, and he trekked the two blocks to the candy counter at Grand Central where he exchanged it for eight pounds of M&M's, a rate of thirty cents per pound. Home was an uphill climb, so he took plenty of breaks on the curb to rest and enjoy the booty. However, the adventure was over when his mother drove up and took him into custody, seizing the goods.

Colleen was a classic beauty who kept her hickory brown hair fashionably short and curly. The eldest of six children, she was the source of Lynn's incalculable number of freckles and filled their home with her love of the arts. She played melodies off her piano and carefully painted cherry blossoms and colorful landscapes on the walls. She had a passion for animals since birth, and regularly caught snakes as a young girl, insisting her little sister help despite the protests. Colleen's home and heart were filled with animals throughout her life, and, in her retirement, she maintained a steady stream of Rottweilers and other rescue dogs. Her yard brimmed with flowers and ponds to attract butterflies and honeybees, even becoming a beekeeper herself and sharing her fresh honey with me. My dad, sister, and I joined her in the beekeeping venture years later when he retired, and I have cherished that connection with her. My dad and I cut windows into our hives, covering them in plexiglass and installing tiny doors, so the kids could enjoy watching the bees work without the need for protective suits. Caring for those honeybees turned my daughters from an everything-that-flies-is-scary attitude into insect-loving children.

Lynn shared his mother's love of animals, particularly the unusual ones, a characteristic nurtured by both of his parents. On a trip home from Texas, Don was driving down the highway when an armadillo puttered onto the road. Don swerved and successfully missed it but quickly pulled over, captured it, and brought it home. Lynn named it Stompy and was fascinated when it would jump straight into the air, hitting the wood at the top of his crate. Whenever it played outside, Lynn enjoyed following its tracks where it dragged its nose through the dirt, sniffing its way around. One fateful day it escaped, but Lynn continued to find new holes in the yard long afterward.

Don and Colleen's marriage rarely saw smooth sailing, and, at the tipping point, Colleen took Don's hunting rifles and smashed them into the concrete floor of their garage, giving the barrels a significant crook. Deciding it was time to throw in the towel, they gathered the children together and announced they were getting a divorce. At eleven years old and the eldest of the kids, Lynn took the news the hardest. Soon Colleen moved out, and a year later, Lynn was faced with the prospect of leaving everything he had known. Don was moving himself and the kids to Salt Lake City, but Lynn wanted to remain at his school and asked to stay behind. Don agreed and Lynn moved back in with his grandparents, Marlow and Leone, this time sharing the basement with his uncle George. The ceiling was low, making them wary of hitting their heads on the sewer pipes.t The ground kept the rooms cool, and it was where Leone kept her endless bottles of canned apricots, peaches, and apples.

Leone was a captivating storyteller and a healthy balance against her husband's unrestrained generosity. Marlow would offer his kids the moon while Leone would say, "After your chores are done." If the kids ever asked Marlow for a dollar, he'd give them five, and if they asked him for five, he'd give them ten. His life's pursuit was to become a doctor, but he could not afford medical school, so he became the next best thing—a pharmacist. A book often read in their home said, "I have lotions and potions and powders and pills. I have all kinds of cures for all manner of ills."

The kids and grandkids regularly received shots, and they knew if they ever coughed in his presence, they'd get at least one more. His son, Paul, remembers having more holes in his rear than a sieve. Marlow had a shot for everything. He believed in medicine. He took so much of it himself; the family was surprised they even needed to embalm him when he died. He told them, "I've worked in Nile Products so long, stood in so much formaldehyde, they can just take me to the grave. Don't even bother embalming me."

The west end of the kitchen contained the Fisher home pharmacy and remedy shop. Most nights when the telephone rang, it would be the cracked voice of an elderly woman. "Is Marlow there?" The kids knew what would come next. "Have you got my pills? Can you tell him to come to see me when he gets home?" Marlow was a doctor from day one, housed in the body of a pharmacist.

STEEP TERRAIN

When Lynn turned sixteen and earned his driver's license, his grandfather hired him to make "fluid trips," delivering formaldehyde and other embalming chemicals to local mortuaries. It was an eerie job, made worse because he was required to walk through the back door where the bodies were. Much like the Culligan Man, Lynn would bring full jugs of embalming fluid to customers and retrieve the empty ones. He then carted the empty jugs down the road to a local farm called Smoot Dairy where the owner washed them in his automated washing machine and put them back in boxes to be filled again. "I don't think washing milk jars and formaldehyde in the same equipment would go over well these days," my dad told me.

With Lynn doing well in school, his parents asked him to use his influence over Mark to help him improve his grades. Lynn gladly agreed and drove across town to his dad's house.

"Hey Mark, come hang out with me," he said to his now sixteen-year-old brother. The two stepped out the front door and followed the walkway to the curb where an envy-inducing 1967 maroon Camaro sat.

"Oh man, your car is the greatest!" Mark said. "Have you been doing any more work to it?"

"Yeah, I just put in a 400ci engine."

"No way!" he said, running around the side and opening the passenger door. Sliding onto the soft leather seat, Mark took a deep breath, inhaling the sweet smell of gasoline that clings to the inside of muscle cars.

"Here's the deal, Mom and Dad want me to help you get your grades up, so I'm going to make you an offer. If you buckle down on your schoolwork and make Mom and Dad happy, I'll let you borrow my Camaro to take a girl on a date."

"DONE!"

"Good. Now let's go for a ride." Lynn turned the key, and the engine roared to life. As they pulled away from their side street, Mark hit the radio, and they spent the rest of the evening cruising through town and listening to the Kinks and the Rolling Stones.

"I was a good kid in high school," my dad told me, "but there was one story my parents never found out about, even to this day. It was the end of a Friday night football game, and ten of my buddies and I were still wound up and ready for excitement. We headed to the police station and taped the swinging front doors shut to buy us some time so we could let the air out of the tires on the police cruisers and toilet-paper the parking lot. What we didn't realize was the fact that the front doors swung both ways, not one way like we had thought, and the police came flying out of the station before we could all get away.

We ran like bats out of Hell but didn't realize some of our friends had been caught until we had reached a safe place and noticed some of us were missing. We obviously didn't have the smarts of career criminals because we made the mistake of returning to the scene of the crime to look for our friends. That's when we were nabbed. All eleven of us were tossed into jail and left to sit there for three hours while we contemplated our poor choices. After a while, parents began showing up to haul their kids home, but I was one of three in the group who had already turned eighteen and was not required to phone home. When I finally made it home to my grandparent's house that night, I decided to take the story to my grave."

During this time, Lynn decided he needed braces but knew he would need to pay for them himself. At the time, he figured the difference between a good orthodontist and a cheap one was the level of pain he would have to endure, so he made an appointment with the least expensive doctor he could find and went in for his new braces. The man was in his retirement years, and his assistant was his elderly wife. As the man worked to install the braces, his tools kept hitting the roof of Lynn's mouth and were causing a lot of bleeding. The doctor was progressively getting more frustrated and kept yelling at his wife who was attempting to soak up the blood. Eventually, the man began throwing the blood-soaked cotton swabs at the wall before finally finishing the procedure.

As Lynn left the office and took the elevator to the first floor, one of the bands popped off his new braces. Lynn knew he would have to return and reluctantly headed back to the doctor once more. The man immediately accused him of eating the wrong food even though Lynn didn't even have time to leave the building. He began searching for a better orthodontist, and each one immediately recognized the handiwork the moment Lynn opened his mouth. Unfortunately, Lynn could not afford the further treatment, so he went home and yanked it all off with a pair of pliers.

8

Widowmaker

Overlooking a prison at the base of the Salt Lake Valley was an internationally infamous ridge considered to be one of the toughest tracks in the world. It struck fear into anyone who attempted to scale it and drew fans and competitors from around the globe. At a thousand feet high, the last two hundred feet were practically a vertical cliff. Motorcycles had been the only vehicles capable of scaling its rocky face, and, out of the many who attempted it, only three had ever made it over the top.

The annual "Hill Climb" brought national television coverage, and Lynn was asked to give a pre-race demonstration. "This ridge has never been attempted in a four-wheeled vehicle," Lynn said. "But I'm going to show you just how steep it is." With that, he climbed into his Jeep and turned the engine over. As he pulled up to the threshold at the base, he tried to hush the mental image of his Jeep rolling end over end. This wasn't a speed race, and the ridge needed to be conquered with strategy. As he started his ascent, the track grew steeper and steeper, dirt spitting out from under his struggling tires. The tall sagebrush scraped the sides of his Jeep, and he soon maxed out at the eight-hundred-foot mark. He put his vehicle in reverse and began carefully backing down the mountain to the reporters. Affirming what he already knew, he assured them, "No four-wheeled vehicle will ever reach the top of this ridge. Only a motorcycle would have a chance."

When race weekend came, the two-day event was split by vehicle prowess. Saturday consisted of small-engine Jeeps, and, although they demonstrated impressive talent, none of them could reach Lynn's previous mark. The second day brought bigger engines, but it had snowed the previous night, and wind gusts had created steep snowbanks against the mountain. However, the weather hadn't deterred the crowds, and the volume of attendees was so immense that the main freeway couldn't handle the traffic coming off the ramp.

Lynn wasn't in the habit of warming any benches, so he put his name on the roster for another attempt. When it was his turn and he rolled up to the base, he gently pulsed the accelerator and began his climb again. Building momentum up the steep slope, he was ecstatic when he surpassed his previous 800-foot mark, and he fought to maintain traction as he climbed even higher. The sheer incline was now nearly vertical, and his speed had slowed to a crawl. Unable to advance any further, he held the brake to prevent a backward roll.

As he clung to the side of Widowmaker's ledge, he could sense the danger of how high he was, but the fog prevented him from seeing the base. The crowd had quickly lost sight of him as he ascended the mountainside and now had to keep track of him by listening to the sound of his engine. After a moment, someone called out to him, "Do you want to back down the mountain or take the winch over the top?"

"For Heaven's sake, I'll take the winch!"

The unexpected success of his last attempt drove him to try a third time. At a time when everyone else was driving like it was a drag race and spinning out halfway up, Lynn idled off the line and simply drove, rather deliberately, straight up the mountain. Much to everyone's shock, this time he sailed over the top. Lynn couldn't believe he had accomplished what he, himself, had declared impossible. Only a handful of nationally-ranked hillclimbers had ever reached the top, and now he was the first to do it on four wheels. Lynn held that record for decades because not long after, Widowmaker was closed. Its landowner knew it was only a matter of time before it lived up to its name, so he had it shut down after twenty-five years of nail-biting stunts. The mountain was closed, and hill-climbing enthusiasts around the nation mourned its loss.

Lynn's last day in the world of racing was a top fuel drag competition in Montreal, Canada. He had been anticipating another sand race but was surprised to find the terrain was more like dirt, giving it a significantly different kind of traction. The competition was going to be tough against a home team of competitors already familiar with the local turf, but Lynn focused on another win. His pit crew pushed his racer up to the starting mark and performed a final check. Lynn glanced over at the racer next to him and sized up his dragster.

Lynn fixed his eyes on the Christmas tree, and the crew backed up. It was time to rock and roll. Yellow. Yellow. Yellow. Green. He smashed the accelerator, and his tires spun forward in a fury. However, the tiny wheelie bars protruding from the back weren't strong enough to prevent the front end from popping up, and the nose went soaring into the air. Lynn held back the nitro, knowing the race was already lost. The nose came down with a hard smash, and Lynn cringed over the damage it must have taken.

The crew helped him haul it back to the pit area where Lynn walked around his red beauty, running his fingers over the dents in the body. He inspected the structural frame and knew it was going to need a lot of work. Racing was a passion he had poured his life into, but now he felt ready to move on. He sold the car right on the spot. "That's when I got into airplanes," he said.

....

"Hand me Casey," Keith said, reaching for the urn in the co-pilot's seat. Lynn slowed the plane as they neared the skies over Alta's steepest, thrill-inducing slope. The High Rustler was a straight run over a thousand feet to the base and a favorite for its airtime opportunities. Looking down over the resort, Lynn could see a mapping of Alta's intertwining ski runs, lined by thousands of green spruce and fir trees.

"We're almost there," he shouted over the rumble of the engine and rushing wind. Lynn was still in shock over the suicide of his fellow Alta buddy and ski instructor, Casey, but when Lynn and Keith heard Casey had wanted his ashes spread over his favorite ski run, the two quickly stepped up. They were now flying high in Lynn's turbo-charged Piper Arrow when they should have rented something slower. As they approached the run, the plane was still going too fast, so Lynn lowered the flaps, landing gear, and everything else he could think of to give them some drag.

"Okay, we're over High Rustler," Lynn called out.

"I can't get the urn open! It's stuck!" Keith said.

"Keeping trying, I'll make another pass."

"Never mind, it was upside down."

Once turned right side up, the urn popped open without a problem, and the plane closed in for a second attempt. Lynn, again, tried to slow it as much as possible, but it was still moving too fast for their task at hand. Keith pulled the door open and held it with his foot, letting a gust of biting wind roar through the cabin.

"Ready!" Lynn shouted, and Keith threw the ashes out the door. Anticipating a stream that gently showered down across the mountain, they were shocked when the wind and air pressure sucked the entire jar's worth of ashes back inside the plane. It filled the cabin and got stuck in their hair, noses, and teeth. As well-intended as Lynn and Keith were in their attempt to give Casey an honorable wake, his ashes ended up in a vacuum back at the airport.

It wasn't long into Lynn's time at Alta that he got the bug for flying. A fellow patrolman named Mike Scott had been looking to get a pilot's license and had talked Lynn into taking lessons as well. They arranged a regular schedule with their instructor and worked exceptionally hard. When Lynn was called to do his first solo flight, it scared him to death. However, much to his delight, he survived. Once they both achieved their license, Lynn and Mike went in together to purchase a plane. It was a single-prop

Piper Warrior with yellow and blue pinstripes. Considered the perfect beginner plane, it was slow as could be, sat up to five people, and did not have retractable landing gear. The wings were low and were used as a step to reach the door of the cockpit.

It was less than a year later that Lynn began looking for an upgrade, and this time he went in on one with a neurologist friend and another buddy from the ski patrol. The new turbo-charged Piper Arrow had retractable landing gear and a sleek, streamlined shape. This would be the plane my dad would take Alyssa and me up in, enjoying the magnificent world of physics before vomiting into our barf bags.

While standing in the hanger and performing a pre-flight check, Lynn noticed the plane's key looked much like the ones found in a lawnmower, missing the complexity of a house or car key. Lynn and the neurologist wanted to test a hunch, so they walked over to the adjacent hanger where a few beach craft planes sat. They climbed inside, and Lynn inserted the key. The plane fired right up.

While Alyssa and I were little girls, our dad took us up for thrills in this Piper Arrow, and Zero-G's were his thing. He would help lift us onto the wing, and the three of us would climb into the five-seater cabin, sometimes bringing one of our Great Danes or our chocolate lab, Willie T. Bone.

"Buckle up!" my dad said, looking back to check our lap belts. With my mother's susceptibility to motion sickness, she stayed firmly on the ground at home. As we took off for the skies, it took a few more minutes before we could reach the necessary altitude and the real fun could begin. Once we were high enough, my dad revved the engine and dropped the nose into a dive. It felt like

STEEP TERRAIN

we were falling out of the sky when my dad suddenly pulled the controls back and sent us into a steep climb. Up and up we'd go, anxiously anticipating what awaited us at the peak. As he leveled us off into a plateau, everyone and everything in the plane started to float.

"Unbuckle, girls!" he called, and we hastily removed our seatbelts for the full effect of the anti-gravity. Our extra sweaters, a few food wrappers, and the two of us would lift off our seats and float around just like we had seen astronauts do on the Discovery Channel. The only difference was we had a dog. It was funny to watch him float around too, completely bewildered by the experience.

These gravity-defying thrills didn't last long before we were pulled back into our seats by gravity, but my dad was always ready to pull us into the next one. Back down we went until we built enough speed to go careening for the skies above us once more. After several roller coasters' worth of glorious hangtime, we called it a day, but not before Alyssa and I lost our last meal. It was always worth it.

"Girls, did I tell you why every Scottish airstrip has a pub?" he asked us as we flew back to the airport.

"No," we replied together.

"It's in case there's ever bad weather and a pilot can't fly, he might as well drink. A jet pilot once told me about an especially foggy night where the air was so thick that the planes had to be grounded. A group of pilots was kicking back with a round of pints when they heard the faint hum of a single-engine aircraft overhead. The men popped their heads out the door and listened as something circled in for a landing. Out of the mist appeared a small plane that touched down on the blacktop. Watching with growing curiosity, the men saw a pilot jump down, unzip his pants, and take a leak. When the man finished, he hopped back in and took off, never to be seen again. This mysterious man was forever named the Phantom Pisser."

Me with my dad's Piper Arrow

9

Frozen Stiff

The river was fifty degrees Fahrenheit. That's butt-puckering level cold. Frigid enough to put someone into Cold Shock if they got thrown in without protection and would eventually overwhelm their body into a heart attack or unconsciousness. It was early May, and Lynn and most of the guys at Alta were sick of the snow, so they drove to Colorado for a kayaking trip on the Dolores River. The weather was going to be sunny and warm, or so the news report said, but they knew the river would be cold because it was fed entirely by melting ice and snow from the mountains.

They pulled into the small town of Dove Creek and made their way to the access ramp. It was surrounded by tall cliffs, red rock plateaus, and endless sagebrush, looking more like a set from an "Old West" cowboy film. The group dumped their camping gear into a raft and climbed into a set of kayaks. As they pushed off from the bank, Lynn gazed at the dramatic scenery and listened to the mellow sapping of the river licking the shore. His kayak rocked peacefully with the flowing river, and it wasn't long before the landscape changed from Old West to a ponderosa forest. The pine trees seemed to reach the sky, and a light covering of pine grass blanketed the ground.

"We should make camp here, guys," said Doug Christenson.

"Sounds good to me," Lynn replied with the rest of the guys.

Lynn paddled to shore and attempted to pry himself from the rubber seal that wrapped around his waist. He pulled his tent from Doug's raft and began piecing it together, looking forward to a good night's sleep. A couple of the other guys built a fire and began cooking some grub for dinner. Lynn could hear it sizzling next to the hot coals and could smell the savory aroma as it drifted through camp.

"Dinner's up! Come and get it."

Lynn filled his tin bowl and shook some pepper over the top as it steamed. He picked a nearby spot and sat on a log as everyone gathered to enjoy the warmth of the fire.

"Do you guys remember that time Doug leg wrestled an Episcopalian priest?" Lynn asked.

"Don't you tell that story," Doug said.

"Oh, we want to hear it!" the others insisted.

"It was this classy restaurant up Middle Creek Canyon called the Panache," Lynn said, "and we were drinking as much as we wanted because my girlfriend half-owned it. The priest, who was a *lady*, challenged Doug to an Indian leg wrestle…"

"A what?" someone asked.

"It's like a thumb war but with your legs. You sit next to each other with your feet out straight, that sort of thing," Doug said.

"So anyway," Lynn continued, "Doug was on the floor of this restaurant, sitting next to a priest, and there wasn't enough room, so we had to move a bunch of dining tables out of the way. As they started grappling, they each tried throwing their leg on top of the other's and holding it down. While we were cheering, the other customers in the room were just trying to have a nice, quiet dinner. After the leg wrestle, the priest challenged him to an arm wrestle, but Doug said, 'Not a chance. I've already been embarrassed enough.'"

"Oh man!" one of the guys said.

"Oh yeah," Doug jumped in, "what about the time you and Bentsen Moss went bow hunting in Skull Valley and ran his Jeep off the road because the two of you were drinking too much."

"No, we were *racing*. We wanted to see what his CJ5 could do and laid it out in the middle of nowhere," Lynn said.

"And then he ran it off the road and busted the steering," Doug said.

"Yeah. We just sat there waiting and hoping someone would come to our rescue."

"Didn't you have to hitchhike out of there?" Doug asked.

"Yep. After a while, we had decided we'd better start walking and made it about seven miles before finding the highway. We stood there for over an hour, hoping to catch the first vehicle that came our way. It was on an Indian reservation, and this one guy came up in a pickup truck. He was pretty reluctant to give us a ride, but he let us jump in the back and took us to a phone booth in Grantsville. By then, it was one o'clock in the morning and the middle of November, so we had to huddle in the phone booth to stay warm. A friend eventually showed up at six o'clock with a flatbed trailer, and we headed out to retrieve the Jeep. That was a long, cold night, and we didn't get home until late afternoon the next day."

"I'm too cold for these stories. Someone talk about hiking in the desert or a beach somewhere," Doug said.

"What about that Alta Halloween party at the Buckhorn where Lynn showed up dressed as a nun?" someone asked.

"What are you talking about? That was a great costume!" Lynn interjected.

"There was a coffee table there with several lines of cocaine, and I took a picture of him holding a straw next to it," they added.

"Even though I didn't do any," Lynn said, "the moment you snapped that picture, I knew I would never be able to hold a public office. Somehow that photo would surface one day."

"No doubt, my friend. No doubt," Doug added.

The next morning, Lynn crawled out of his warm sleeping bag into the frigid air outside and was shocked at what he saw.

"Snow?!" he said, staring at the campsite.

"You've got to be kidding me." another patrolman piped in. "This is what we came here to get away from!"

Lynn grabbed his kayak paddle and began shoveling paths between the tents. The other guys cooked up breakfast while snowflakes continued to fall.

"What do you guys think about holding over today and getting back on the river tomorrow when it's better weather?" Doug asked.

"Amen to that."

"Agreed," Lynn said.

They spent the rest of the day trying to stay warm around the fire, sitting on hot rocks and drinking Southern Comfort. When Lynn and the group emerged from their tents the second morning, they found even more snow.

"No!" someone groaned.

"This has got to be at least three feet deep!" Lynn said.

"There's only one way out of here, and it's downstream," Doug said.

"Tally-ho," said another, half-heartedly. As they loaded the rafts, Lynn walked over to the tree where they had hung their wetsuits to dry during the first day.

"They're frozen solid!" Lynn said, brushing the snow off and trying to pry them off the tree.

"We can thaw them with hot water," Doug said, grabbing a pot and filling it with water from the river. As soon as it started rolling, he carried it over from the fire, and Lynn held his suit out and let the steaming water course down. As the suit began to relax, Lynn attempted to force his legs inside.

"Yeowzer, that's cold!" he said, gritting his teeth and jumping around, trying to squeeze himself in. It wasn't any more pleasant for the rest of the guys to break their way back into the frozen wet suits either. When they finally suited up, Doug jumped into the raft, and the rest boarded their kayaks. They continued down the river and, by mile marker eight, they had left the high Colorado desert and entered the red rock formations of Southern Utah. Lynn felt like he was on an alien planet as he looked over the landscape where filmmakers had created the 1968 *Planet of the Apes.*

The snow continued to cascade down as they reached their first rapids, and Lynn was wishing he had brought his goggles to help him see through the fog, snow, and spray. As they approached a rapid called Snaggletooth, a blockage of large boulders forced the river over the top and sent another layer of mist into the air. Amongst the foaming white water, Lynn's kayak rolled over and plunged him into the bitter cold of the river. Wetsuits don't ease the shock of an initial polar immersion, and Lynn felt the cold like a punch to his gut.

Fully submerged and upside down beneath the kayak, the forceful rapids swirled around him, and he was unable to right himself. As a plan B, he muscled his way out of the kayak's rubber seal and swam to the surface, grabbing the plastic hull. The wet suit soaked up the arctic water like a sponge, but after a few minutes, his body was able to warm it, giving him the protection he desperately needed. He pulled the kayak onto the snow-covered bank, dumped the water from the hull, and squeezed himself back in. He used his paddle to push onto the river and caught back up with the group. For three days, Lynn and his kayak continued to roll until he couldn't take it anymore.

"Doug, can I ride in the raft with you?"
"Sure thing."

Lynn roped his kayak to the back of the raft, and they towed it for the rest of the trip. That night it finally stopped snowing, notably boosting the group's morale. The last day brought rain, but they were happy having reached their destination and pulled up on the Dewey Bridge boat ramp. On their drive back to Salt Lake City, they were gifted a full-scale blizzard. The air was so thick that they had to take turns driving while sticking their heads out the window to see. "This has been a trip to remember," Doug said.

Rafting Trip

10

Nothing But Rubble

"There's been an explosion!" a voice shouted over the radio. "All-hands-on-deck at the Gold Miner's Daughter!" The call came from Doug, who was standing next to the ticket booth and had just finished helping a helicopter with a rescue on the other side of the road. He had heard the explosion and looked up to see debris flying through the air.

It was a Friday at 2 pm in March of 1985, and Lynn had been resting at the top of Alta's mountains. He hadn't heard an explosion, but, upon hearing the cry over the radio, he, Darwon, and a third patrolman pointed their skis toward the base and flew as fast as the wind would carry them. Despite being the farthest away at the time of the incident, they were the first responders to reach the scene. As Lynn surveyed the rubble, he was stunned to see the entire north wing of the three-story lodge was gone. In its place was a war zone of crumbled bricks, and he could taste the dust in the air. Shards of glass covered the parking lot where car windows had been blown out. Suddenly, he heard a feeble cry for help.

"There!" Lynn shouted, directing anyone within earshot to the location of what appeared to be a young girl. He climbed the thirty-foot mound of crumbled concrete as quickly as he could, but his ski boots kept slipping on the dusty surfaces, and it was difficult to avoid getting tangled in the broken and twisted rebar. He reached the girl shortly after Darwon.

"My hand is stuck!" she cried.

"Don't worry, we're going to get you out of here," Lynn assured her, but as he glanced at the mammoth-sized chunk of concrete pinning her hand, he knew this would be no easy task.

"We're going to need more help," Darwon said.

They assessed the girl for signs of trauma and shock, watching for rapid breathing, an accelerated pulse, and enlarged pupils.

"How old are you?" Lynn asked her.

"Twelve. My mother was just with me over in the bathroom. Where did she go?"

"Don't worry, we'll find her," Lynn said as he began scrambling through the rubble. He upturned chunks of cement and pieces of furniture before finally glimpsing a woman's arm.

"I found her!" Lynn called to Darwin. "Quick, help me dig her out!"

The two frantically moved heavy pieces of debris until they uncovered a woman lying in a bathtub. She was weak but conscious.

"Are you okay?" Lynn asked, testing to see if the woman would respond.

"I don't know," she mumbled.

"We're going to help you. We have your daughter, and she's okay." Lynn turned to Darwon, "I'm going to get more help."

As Lynn climbed over more chunks of concrete and bricks, he canvased the wreckage and spotted another woman. Her body was lying partway out of the rubble, and a stillness came over him as he realized she was already dead. Calls went out for every available emergency resource in the area, and, within thirty minutes, twenty-eight doctors, seventeen nurses, and seven paramedics showed up from Snowbird where they had been enjoying a day off. Over two hundred people poured in to help with the rescue effort, and the closest hospital activated a 'mass casualty plan.' Among the newly arrived volunteers was a physician who quickly attended to the twelve-year-old girl. As he inspected her injury and the challenge of releasing her from the concrete slab that pinned her, he warned that he might have to amputate. While he continued to care for her, Lynn proceeded to help her mother through the minefield of unstable ground and into an ambulance.

Alta's own avalanche search and rescue dog was on the scene immediately, followed closely by more rescue dogs brought in for the effort. One of the maids working in the lodge was uncovered after being pinned under the wreckage for over twenty minutes, but she was alive. Before the blast, she had been focused on her duties when a massive gust of wind plowed through the hallway, and everything came down on her. She, too, didn't hear an explosion.

It was now hours into the search, and the temperature was dropping below thirty-two degrees. Chemical heating packs were wrapped around the young girl to stave off hypothermia, but the physician was still worried about her condition and finalized plans for amputation. A surgical tray was requested, and permission was obtained from the mother. The physician examined the girl one last time to see if she could hold on a little longer and was surprised to see what a fighter she was. Instead, he decided to postpone the amputation and recommended the team keep trying to move the concrete slab. A sixty-ton crane was hauled in but they were still unable to free her from the twenty-five-ton chunk of concrete. A beefier 125-ton crane was brought in, finally freeing the young girl, and, after eight hours in the rubble, she was life-flighted to St. Mark's hospital.

With the girl now freed from the debris, volunteers were able to rescue a man trapped underneath her, alive. Miraculously, the girl's hand received no broken bones, and her mother suffered only a fractured hip. A fourth woman survived but was still in critical condition after undergoing eleven hours of surgery. The explosion resulted in two deaths, a marvel considering the extent of the damage. Much of that miracle was attributed to the blue, sunny skies that had drawn the crowds outside and onto the slopes.

Lynn was interviewed that day by Michael Ross of Channel 2 news.

"Did you smell propane before you went in?" he asked.

"No, I didn't smell any propane."

"Have you known anyone that said it smelled like propane?"

"No," Lynn said again.

Despite the cause being an apparent gas leak, Lynn didn't want to give information he didn't have. The cause was later confirmed to be a leak from a large propane tank in the basement, and the news reached as far as the New York Times. Lynn also learned that the walls in the Gold Miner's Daughter were built like a ladder, so when the tank exploded, the walls blew out, sending the floor levels cascading down on top of each other like pancakes, each weighing approximately fifty tons. The roof had lifted four feet before plunging to the ground with the rest of the rubble.

On top of the medical training the patrol maintained, Alta also kept an advanced medical patrol on-call, assisting the rest of the team when needed, particularly when medications like morphine needed to be given. Severe injuries were rare, but morphine was kept on site just in case. "They were handy like that," Lynn said, "and they didn't have to perform the grunt work we did." These docs weren't always available and, according to Lynn, may not have been employees, but rather volunteer medical professionals who offered their services whenever they were on the slopes. Free season passes were likely part of the exchange, and they wore Alta Patrol coats, saving them a wait in the lift line.

As they noticed Lynn's knack for medicine, they told him he should make a career out of it. "You should become a Physician Assistant," they said. Lynn decided to research the job and was immediately intrigued. The position of a PA traditionally entailed working in rural family practice clinics, an attempt to bring health care to harder-to-reach communities. It has since expanded to many realms of medicine, but Lynn liked the thought of moving to a small town and caring for its community. He spoke with several doctors and resident doctors, who each told him Physician Assistants were the ones who taught them everything they knew. Lynn was hooked.

11

Animals of a Different Kind

My parents first met when my dad's flying buddy and fellow patrolman, Mike Scott, invited him to pilot some friends to Jackson Hole, Wyoming.

"We're going cross-country skiing for the weekend, and there will be a new girl coming. If you like her, you can stick around and join us," Mike offered.

"Sounds like a fun time," Lynn said.

On Friday morning, Lynn waited at the airport's hanger for the group to arrive. When Mike and his girlfriend, Mary, showed up, he noticed a beautiful brunette with them. She was slightly shorter than himself and had a bright smile and styled her hair in a feminine pixie cut that subtly hid her ears.

"Lynn, this is Michaela Wheelan," Mike said. "She and Mary were x-ray technicians in San Diego for a few years."

"Everyone calls me Mickey," she said.

"It's great to meet you," Lynn replied, shaking her hand.

They climbed into the plane, and Lynn took his place in the pilot's seat with Mike next to him as his co-pilot. The flight was filled with light-hearted banter, and Lynn took a liking to Mickey's charming and soft-spoken nature. An authentic midwestern girl if there ever was one, he learned she was raised on an Iowa hog farm and grew up alongside her father's cornstalks and fields of soybean.

"We're about to reach the air over Jackson Hole," Lynn called out to the group, "and it's a balmy twenty degrees below zero."

"Last night was recorded at forty degrees below zero," Mike added.

"Holy smokes," Mickey said.

As the sun was dipping behind the trees, the landscape was being blanketed in shadow, and the last remnants of sunlight lit the summit of the Grand Tetons in a breathtakingly orange and pink hue. These mountains are famous for their voluptuously impressive peaks and were named by a group of unquestionably homesick French explorers. The air was exceptionally crisp and clear, and the scene was like an oil painting from a master's canvas.

Lynn, who was not one to miss an opportunity, veered away from the regional airport and headed for the jagged, snow-dusted peaks instead. He knew the laws restricting pilots from flying too close to objects such as radio towers, mountains, and the ground. The Grand Canyon, for instance, cannot be flown over at all, but this didn't stop Lynn from pulling right up alongside the majestic spires and circling them for a full 360-degree view. As he dipped his left wing into the turn, he flew so close that

Mickey thought the tip of the wing was going to scrape the cliffs. He didn't know it yet, but she was smitten.

After making a full circle, Lynn steered the plane back to the regional airport and prepared for landing. When the runway appeared just ahead, Mike turned to Lynn, "So, when are you going to lower the landing gear?"

"Oh! Now. Right now," Lynn said, jumping for the pull lever and yanking it down. Lynn knew the plane had a safety mechanism that would have deployed the wheels at the last second, but it was still a close call. They touched down and noticed the blanket of snow reached higher than the fence posts. The group rented a Landcruiser and spent the weekend cross-country skiing, window shopping in the town square, and dancing at the Million Dollar Cowboy Bar. When they checked into a hotel for the night, Lynn offered to share a room with Mickey, but when she declined, it wasn't in a "No, thank you" kind of way, but more of a "No way in Hell." Lynn liked that about her and brought her a pastry and a cup of coffee the next morning instead.

After returning to Salt Lake City, Lynn took Mickey on two more dates before she returned home to Iowa, and, from then on, Lynn flew to her house once a month to take her out to dinner. Sometimes she was able to visit him in Utah, and on her first visit after Jackson Hole, Lynn took her to Alta's annual spaghetti party held for the patrol at the Alpen Glow restaurant. Located halfway up the mountain, the Alpen Glow cannot be accessed by vehicle and is the hub of hungry skiers wanting to grab a burger in the middle of a day full of sun. The front doors are perpetually surrounded by hundreds of colorful skis where customers stick them in the snow like fence posts. During the party, most of the crowd already had a few drinks when Lynn stood up to make an announcement.

Gesturing to Mickey, he said, "I want you all to know this woman is going to be the mother of my children."

Mickey's bewildered expression mimicked the rest of the room and she felt hot under the stare of every eye in the restaurant. "What??" she thought to herself. An awkward silence had fallen, but, as Lynn sat down, the lively chatter resumed and everyone returned to their spaghetti. When the party was done, everyone clipped back into their skis and headed the rest of the way down the mountain. Lynn watched as one of the guys jumped on a snowmobile and started a game resembling steer wrestling. The man pulled the snowmobile up alongside a skier, jumped off, and tackled them into the snow. Once he could climb back on the snowmobile, he'd pull up alongside another victim and tackle them too. Lynn and many of the others were wearing cross-country skis that day, something they were not as proficient in, making them easy targets.

As Lynn and Mickey's courtship progressed, they attended a wedding reception in Montana for fellow patrolman, Bill Hoffman. Doug tagged along for the flight, and, on the way up, they made a stopover in Pinedale, Wyoming, to meet up with Stuart Thompson in his hometown. As Mickey climbed down from the plane and onto the tarmac of the small, rustic town, a tall man with a handlebar mustache walked up and wrapped her in a hug.

"I just wanted to meet the girl that lassoed Lynn Falkner!" he said.

"Mickey, this is Stuart," Lynn said with a grin. "And this is his wife, Mary," he continued, gesturing to the petite woman next to him. They spent the night dancing at the Stockman's bar, and while the music played, Mickey looked over her shoulder and saw a ragtag man sitting against a wall, looking as if he'd been down a few dirt roads. The man caught her gaze and shifted his eyes to her dancing partner.

"Falkner!" The man shouted from across the room.

"Danny Hittle?!" Lynn exclaimed, spinning around. They exchanged a thorough handshake and pulled in for a hug.

"Mickey, this man used to race Jeeps with me, and printed on the back of his Jeep was the abbreviation 'PFFT,' which stood for 'Pretty F'ing Fast,'" Lynn explained with a laugh.

Mickey now understood the ongoing joke that everywhere Lynn went, he knew someone because, at some point, they met either on the race track or the ski patrol. Although, she quickly learned the wildest characters came from the ski patrol. "They were animals," my dad would tell me with a grin, and my mom would nod in agreement. "One such duo were the brothers Casey and Mike from Bemidji, Minnesota," he told me. "One night at a Wyoming bar, they guzzled too much alcohol, and I watched Casey climb onto the counter and challenge all the cowboys to lasso his feet. Not surprisingly, a man accepted the challenge and quickly caught both Casey's feet and yanked them out from under him like one of the many steers in the man's field. As Casey fell, his hand smashed a shot glass, and the sharp edges punctured an artery and sent blood across the counter." Lynn and the others hauled him away to the emergency room, but it wasn't long after getting stitched up that he found his way right back to the same bar. As Lynn predicted, Casey was forced to return to the ER for a second time that night, no doubt due to more shenanigans.

After the layover in Wyoming, Lynn and Mickey flew the remainder of the way to Montana, and they were looking forward to a fun-filled party. Most of the guys on the Alta patrol would be there, so it was a good bet that things would get a little rowdy. Lynn dropped Mickey off at the airport where a rental car was waiting for her and returned to the skies, this time with Darwon. The fellow patrolman wanted to "make an entrance" in front of their buddies, so they headed up in a high-winged plane and prepped to make a jump. Born and raised in Alaska and having done stunt work for several James Bond films, Darwon Stoneman was one crazy dude.

By law, pilots are required to have special training for sky diving because, without it, nothing is allowed to be thrown from a plane. Not sandbags, balloons, and particularly not people. Lynn expressed his concern, but Darwon assured him that a basic pilot's license would be sufficient. As they approached the designated altitude, Darwon pushed the door open, and a gust of frigid Montana air rushed inside. Clutching the rim of the door, he leaned out and positioned himself by stepping on the landing gear. However, Lynn didn't know to set the brake on the tires, and Darwon's foot spun off, whipping his feet out from under him and sending his face into the wing. Lynn heard a "Wham!" and watched his friend get sucked out into the abyss.

"Did I just kill Darwon?!" Lynn thought. He circled the plane around and strained to see if his buddy was okay. Suddenly, he spotted Darwon free-falling through the skies, but couldn't tell if he was conscious. There was nothing Lynn could do at this point, but he continued to watch over him, hoping at any moment he would pull his parachute and Lynn would know he was okay. When the parachute finally inflated, Lynn let out a full sigh of relief and turned for the airport. When Lynn made it to the reception, he could see Darwon had been banged up for sure, but he had made his grand entrance just fine.

Back home at Alta, Lynn, Mickey, and several others were enjoying the rooftop pool at the Cliff Lodge in Snowbird. The water was heated to compete against the cold, winter air, and the lounge chairs were often topped in a layer of snow instead of towels. Doug was wearing a pink Speedo and everyone had just come from a bar at the Keyhole Mexican restaurant where they had been drinking margaritas by the pitcher. As the situation got a little rowdy, Mickey encouraged Lynn to leave before things got out of hand. "She was good for him," Doug later recalled.

It was a good thing she did, because that's when Howie and Casey decided to go downstairs and show the pretentious-looking valet drivers how to properly dress. The Cliff Lodge was known for the uniforms they put their valet in, with their long, winter coats and tall hats that made them look like Russian escorts. Howie and Casey stripped down to nothing and began acting like valet drivers. Wearing nothing but their shoes, they quickly approached new customers and asked for their keys, which were handed over before the customers realized what the men were, or *weren't*, wearing. By the time it registered, Howie was pressing his cheeks to their seats and driving away. The whole group was kicked out of the lodge, but Howie and Casey were worried they would be arrested. They quickly got dressed and grabbed some pine tree branches along the tree line and stuffed them into the back of their pants. In their more-than-slightly inebriated minds, they would camouflage into the landscape as they snuck back to Alta.

While I sat in my dad's living room, listening to him tell these stories, I was reminded that his life seemed to have two vastly different eras, a wild time of risk-taking before he met my mother, and a steady, polished life after. My mother appeared to be the catalyst in the change, but I would later understand it was not as clear-cut of a transition as I had thought. However, it was always a good laugh when my dad told stories of when those two worlds had collided.

Years after the naked valet incident, Lynn invited a neurosurgery colleague to the Steak Pit at Snowbird to introduce him to a few Alta patrol friends, including "Hambone Jr."

"Howie, this is my friend and colleague from the children's hospital, Dr. Steege," Lynn said, gesturing to his friend. Howie's jovial attitude disappeared, and his expression turned stone cold. He then threw himself forward and slammed his face into his food, much to the bewilderment of everyone at the table. Lynn turned to see his colleague's face, nervous about what he must be thinking. The doctor returned the glance with a startled expression that seemed to say, "Nice friends, Lynn."

Lynn and Mickey met in February, and by May, he had asked her to dinner at the prestigious La Caille restaurant in the Salt Lake Valley. As they walked along the stone pathway and left the bustle of the city behind, they passed through a grove of trees and long rows of grapevines belonging to the restaurant's in-house winery. The walkway led to an elegant chateau that looked as if it was plucked right from a French hillside. It served only the finest French and Belgian fare, and, as they entered, a server dressed as an authentic wench led them to a table on the second floor. She wore an ornate gold corset over a knee-length black chemise and presented their elegantly simple menu. The sound of clinking wine glasses filled the room and they heard the occasional "Oo" and "Ah" whenever a patron's brandy-covered ice cream was lit aflame.

Lynn and Mickey chatted as they enjoyed each delicious course that came and went. Not long into their dinner, Lynn pulled a small ring box from his pocket and presented it to Mickey. As she opened it, she saw a single diamond displayed inside. Lynn had known a friend who dealt in diamonds and had encouraged Lynn to buy one. It had a strong yellow hue, but the man insisted it was "prestigious." It wasn't mounted to a ring, and the thought of marriage had not yet crossed his mind, but Mickey interpreted the gesture as a proposal, understandably so.

"Yes!" she said, smiling.

Lynn realized the honest misinterpretation but jumped on board with the decision. He was happy to leave bachelorhood behind and felt ready to take the next step in life, especially with a woman like Mickey.

While the two began planning a wedding, they knew they would eventually have to address an elephant in the room. Lynn had been keeping a pet anaconda at home, but Mickey was no fan of snakes. Called Badmouth, Lynn coined the name when he first opened the shipping crate and the snake bit him on the forehead. He chalked it up to being agitated after a long flight, being cooped up in a box, and not having had much handling in general. "After that, he was a pretty nice snake," Lynn said.

In a strange turn of events, the problem solved itself when the snake died in what some might call a freak accident. The pet store had run out of bunnies for the snake's dinner, so Lynn had to come home with a rat instead. When the snake thought it had killed its meal, he happily wolfed it down, but, somehow, the ferocious rat survived and chewed its way out from the inside, killing the snake. Lynn was furious, took his archery bow, and shot at the rat. The arrows just bounced off the rat's body and made both Lynn and the rat angrier. Lynn grabbed his rifle and used the bayonet to stab the vermin and end it for good. Even though it didn't bring his snake back, Lynn figured it at least made Badmouth feel better.

Other than Nero the Boxer, Lynn's pets were not among the usual. His favored dogs were Great Danes, a majestic breed accurately represented by the scared-of-his-own-shadow Scooby-Doo. Since their lifespan is naturally half that of other breeds, our family had a lot of them over the years. It wasn't unusual for drivers to pull over to see the "baby horse" in our pasture, mixed in among the real horses. My parents often took the Danes backpacking in the stunningly beautiful Uinta Mountains, and each had their own saddle bag to carry dog food and supplies.

When my sister and I were kids, our family was invited to a co-worker's ranch where we met the Duke of Earl, a fawn-colored Dane who enjoyed chasing jackrabbits through the hills of sagebrush. When he stood on his back legs and put his paws on my dad's shoulders, his head reached over my dad's, reaching almost six feet tall. It was love at first sight, and my dad jokingly told his friends, "If you ever lose the farm, we'll take the dog." A while later, Duke was brought to our door. They had lost the farm, but we gained the best dog we ever had.

Then there was a tarantula named Digger, given to him as a Valentine's Day gift by an old girlfriend. As my dad struggled to get used to it, he looked at pictures and watched videos of people letting their tarantulas walk over their chests and arms, but my dad couldn't bring himself to do it. He knew he would at least have to move the spider to clean its terrarium, so he strapped ski goggles to his face and pulled thick, winter gloves over his hands for protection. As he slowly reached into the tank, the normally motionless spider flinched. "Nope! That's it! I'm done." He found it another home, far away.

The patty didn't fall far from the cow when it came to Alyssa and me. We both tend to want to house the oddest of creatures, and I often research feasible ways to raise opossums or adopt a raccoon. "Wouldn't it be fun!" I often tell my family, pushing aside the reality of constant kitchen raids and waking up in the middle of the night to a pair of glowing eyes staring at me from the edge of my bed. It's perfectly legal to own a pet raccoon in the state where I live, but, if it weren't, I know I'd be looking to certify as a wildlife rehabilitator. My husband is usually the voice of reason, and I try to remember my mother's wise words, "You need to let that idea go."

I also love the idea of running a beefalo ranch and, for those of you who have never heard of such an animal, it's a cross between a buffalo and a cow. They look exactly like what you'd expect, but their temperament will lean one way or the other.

They can be mild-mannered like a cow or dangerously aggressive like a buffalo. Possibly the inspiration for such a fantasy was my high school's mascot. To fuel our school's buffalo pride, a real buffalo was ridden by one of the students through our homecoming parade and then across the football field to celebrate the start of Friday night's game. It was heroes like that who taught me we are limited only by our imagination. Not to mention, my dad echoed that philosophy my entire life.

My sister opts for unusual dogs, like her Chihuahua-Pug mix that resembles a gremlin, complete with a snaggle tooth and prominent underbite. To solidify the analogy, whenever it gets wet, a change falls over it that can only be described as demonic possession, running around the house and snarling as it attacks blankets and smashes its already flat face into the couch. I was elated to discover the same love of strange pets in my eight-year-old daughter, Claire, when she adopted the leftover worms from our latest fishing trip. She decided they needed a more comfortable home than the small carton I purchased them in from the gas station, and I came home to find an entire fridge crisper drawer filled with dirt from the garden. Not surprisingly, many of the worms had escaped and found their way to every corner of the refrigerator. I laughed it off, just like my dad would have done, and apologized to my daughter that we couldn't keep a drawer full of dirt in the fridge, nor allow the worms to live amongst our food. Despite a thorough deep cleaning, I continued to find worms for another two weeks.

A couple of days later, I was taking formal photos of Claire in the backyard when she asked to take some with her worms. Seeing both myself and my dad in those hopeful eyes made me proud beyond words. "Absolutely!" I told her and dashed off to retrieve them. As we continued with the photoshoot, she stood there in her beautiful, white gown posing for her baptismal invitations while holding a fistful of worms outstretched to the camera. Her eyes glowed with joyful admiration for her little friends, and I will treasure those photos forever.

When Alyssa and I were in the fourth grade, our class incubated a batch of chicken eggs that hatched fluffy, yellow chicks for us to name and swoon over. When the science project was done, my dad offered to keep them since our family lived on rural property and already had chickens. Our favorite from the group was a white rooster whom my sister and I named White Chick. The name sounds politically incorrect now, but I assure you my sister and I were only aware of the fact that he was a chick and his breed was a White Leghorn.

He grew up to be more like a cat and, despite having talons the size of an eagle's, he was the perfect pet. He sat on the fence post by our bus stop and waited for us to return from school every day. As I would hop off the bus, I would scoop him up and carry him everywhere. If I was in the house and he wanted to play, he would fly up on the porch rail and crow until we picked him up once more. When he was eight years old, we noticed his foot had become swollen, so my dad made an appointment with our vet, Dr. Gary Gowans.

As a vet tech led us into an exam room, Alyssa lowered White Chick onto the stainless-steel table and steadied him over the slippery surface. He was nervous being in unfamiliar surroundings, so she slowly stroked the back of his neck, a move we knew to be his kryptonite or Vulcan death grip. The longer she stroked, the lower his head dipped until we heard the "dink" of his beak hitting the table. He was in a deep sleep when Dr. Gowans walked in, but the sound of the door swinging open brought him back to the land of the living.

"Have you ever had a chicken as a patient before?" my dad asked.

"This is my first one!" Gary beamed. After a thorough examination, he prescribed our rooster hour-long soaks in Epsom salt three times a day until the swelling went down. When we got home, we filled my mother's cooking pot with warm, salty water and plopped the chicken in like he was dinner. We plopped the pot on the living room floor and kept him company while playing Monopoly and other board games. After two days of treatments, his foot returned to normal, and he was back to ruling the roost.

Alyssa and I loved animals, even the dead ones. When our dad taught us how to fish, it was like the blind leading the blind as we had little success catching anything in wild streams and lakes. Instead, he took us to hatcheries, where we quickly caught a bucket full of rainbow trout with just a hook and reel, no bait necessary. The best part was getting them home and dressing the fish up in clothes from our Barbie dolls. The outfits never quite fit since the fish had wider waistlines, but they still looked fabulous in their new cocktail dresses. Each time my sister and I finished playing for the evening, we put the fish back in the freezer for the next day.

Alyssa and I with our trout. I am the one shoving it in my mouth.

12

Reverend Vincent Price

As guests gathered in the rustic, wooden chapel of Our Lady of the Snows Catholic Church, Lynn stood by the altar, waiting for the moment Mickey would walk down the aisle. Wearing a grey tux and a black bow tie, he cleaned up nice, but it would be the last time he ever wore a mustache. Behind him, a window stretched from the floor to the ceiling of the A-frame roofline and revealed the majestic snow-covered mountains of Alta. A man playing guitar and another playing the fiddle sat in the corner, providing a background serenade. Lynn's father, Don, stood next to him as the best man, and his brother, Mark, a groomsman.

Hambone took his job seriously as the official usher. When seating in the small chapel filled to capacity, he walked out the door and began waving people away. Guests stood bewildered on the long, snow-covered staircase. "We're full!" he called out, but Lynn rushed to intervene.

"No, let them in, Hambone. We'll make room," he said.

When it was time to begin the nuptials, Hambone stepped up to settle the chatter. "EVERYONE SHUT UP!" he yelled across the room.

"Hambone, shh. It's okay," Lynn said amongst the chuckling guests.

As the bridal procession began, Mickey appeared on her father's arm wearing a white, ankle-length gown layered in Chiffon and holding a bouquet of autumn-inspired flowers. Her eyes beamed as she watched Lynn smiling back, and she gracefully made the walk to the alter. She was exquisite with only a touch of makeup to highlight her natural beauty and a wreath of small white flowers in her hair.

Mickey's father, Mike Wheelan, was a tall, clean-cut man who wore his Irish heritage with pride. He donned freshly ironed slacks and a shirt whenever he drove "into town" for groceries and a suit to Mass every Sunday. A veteran of a Naval supply ship during WWII, he was a man of few words, but his quiet smile spoke volumes. As Mike presented his daughter's hand to Lynn, he stepped to the side, and the Episcopal priest began the ceremony. The priest, whose voice sounded eerily like the actor Vincent Price, the king of black-and-white horror films, also happened to be the father of the wildest man on the Alta patrol, Howie.

Lynn and Mickey were pronounced man and wife, and everyone headed to the Rustler's Lodge for a lively reception. Lynn's grandparents, Marlow and Leone, seemed a little overwhelmed by the band, dancing, wild men, and eating raw hamburger, but were gracious and supportive. In the crowd was Gordy Alcott, a tall patrolman with a big smile who liked grabbing lady's knees and giggling. Whenever he went missing while working the slopes with the team, the other guys knew right where to find him. He'd be curled up, fast asleep, in a lift tower shed or down a tree well where the snow melts away. Despite the narcolepsy, he was the most cheerful man on the team.

Lynn and Mickey spent their honeymoon on the beaches of Kauai, Hawaii, and Mickey was nervously anticipating a diving experience in the ocean like Lynn had spoken so much about. As they prepped their scuba gear in the shell-lined sand, Lynn explained he had never been diving directly off a beach since divers typically take boats far past the breaking waves. Lynn was excited to try something new, so the two suited up in the golden sand, strapping oxygen tanks to their backs and checking gauges. As they entered the wave-cracking shore, it was more brutal than Lynn anticipated, and they had to battle a long distance before it was deep enough to dive under the rough swells. Sandy grit scratched their skin like sandpaper, and the power of the waves pushed them in every direction.

By the time they reached calmer waters, Mickey was beaten up, exhausted, and queasy. Lynn convinced her if they dove down, she'd lose her nausea and everything would be better, so they dropped below the surface and descended into a vibrant world of sea life. The ocean was brimming with colorful fish, and more poured from every crevasse in the coral. The sun's rays filtered down in bands of light that played across the sand, and a current gently carried them from one vivid scene to the next. It was like traveling to another world, offering freedom from gravity and surrounding them in peaceful tranquility. Lynn imagined this was what being in outer space must be like.

Amongst the sea life, Lynn spotted a small shark and quickly turned to Mickey and used his hands to motion, "Little. Shark." She nearly jumped out of her skin, but it wasn't from joy. Throughout the dive, she stuck by Lynn's side, keeping a half pace behind him as they cruised along the reef. When Lynn remembered to check the oxygen levels on his tank, he reached back to retrieve the air pressure gauge, but it was mysteriously stuck. He tugged several more times before giving it one good yank, which set it free. When he pulled it around to read it, he realized what he had been yanking on wasn't his pressure gauge at all. He had ripped Mickey's regulator right out of her mouth. He quickly returned her air supply after realizing what he had done and gave her a moment to recover. She motioned to him that she had had enough, and Lynn agreed, "Okay, we can go back."

As they began their return to shallow waters, Lynn offered to let Mickey relax on the surface while he pulled her towards the shore. Tired and ready to be on land, she welcomed the suggestion. When they neared the beach, the coral rose higher, and Lynn was cautiously trying not to drag Mickey across it. Suddenly, Lynn saw a large moray eel in their way and worried she would swim right into it. These menacing-looking eels were the inspiration for the movie franchise, *Alien* with their second set of jaws that can shoot from deep within their throat to clamp down on prey and pull it into their bellies. Lynn could see each one of its needle-sharp teeth as its mouth gaped open, sucking in water as it breathed. Worried about an imminent collision, he quickly thrust Mickey out of the way without having time to explain. She cleared the eel but was completely bewildered by Lynn's inexplicable behavior and frantically swam back in a panic, returning to the spot he had attempted to avoid. He couldn't stop feeling sorry for the eel and was sure she had put a knee right in its face.

When the trip came to an end and they returned home, it was the end of the winter season, and Hambone brought his annual load of laundry to wash. Lynn was sure it was the only time it got washed. The pants could stand up on their own, and there was a sheen on them from blowing his nose into his hands and wiping them on his pants. He never stayed overnight except for one occasion when they invited him to stay for a few days over Halloween while they went out of town. When the doorbell rang on Halloween night and the neighborhood kids said, "Trick or Treat!" he'd yell four-letter words and "GET OUT OF HERE!" It took a few years for the trick or treaters to muster the courage to come back. Hambone might have been missing a few bricks, but there never was a more loyal friend.

In addition to Hambone, the newlyweds also invited Howie to stay for a couple of weeks while he recovered from a bilateral hernia. It caused significant swelling to his testicles, but he kept asking girls from Alta to come down and see him. He would pull down his pants and say, "Look at these! I mean, I'm tellin' ya!"

He even pulled out the family jewels for Mickey, who responded, "Oh Howie, please no!"

Now having jumped the broomstick into marriage, Lynn felt ready to pursue his career in medicine, something that would provide for the family they were building. MEPCO was doing well after being returned to the stewardship of his father and brother, Mark, and now that Lynn was retired from racing, the company's funds were no longer flying out the door faster than chili cheese dogs on game day. It was time to head back to school, but Lynn knew he would need help making it through the acceptance process into the Physician Assistant program. So, it was time to join the Navy.

13

The Bottom Scratcher

His name was Company Commander Garcia. A man of short stature, this Filipino compensated by sheer volume and, like most drill sergeants, excelled in fuming screams and excessive vocabulary. He struggled to pronounce several English words, and Lynn often heard phrases like, "You mudda puckers! I mash you, you puke!" Lynn wasn't always sure what the man was saying, but he knew it wasn't good. He never had to go to the "sandbox," and didn't know what it meant to become a "sugar cookie," but he knew he didn't want to. Garcia often played "Earth Angel" by The Penguins and sang along as it rolled over and over on repeat for hours. Life under Garcia's command was a mind game to test if Lynn had the salt.

Basic training at the San Diego Naval Training Center began with a bang. Entering as a thirty-seven-year-old member of the enlisted, Lynn was significantly older than most other recruits. He was assigned to Company 927 and was led into his new barracks, a grey room with slick floors and two long rows of beds. Squished between each was a shoulder-high shelf for two recruits to share, and resting on the mattresses were white linens and brown towels folded to perfection. The young man standing next to the bunk adjacent to Lynn's stuck out his arm for a handshake.

"My name's Neal Farwell. It looks like I'm your new bunkmate."

"Pleased to meet you; I'm Lynn Falkner."

"What brought you to the Navy, Falkner?"

"The goal is medicine. I'm trying to get into PA school and heard getting experience as a corpsman will give me the edge I need."

Two other guys walked over, and Neal introduced them. "This is Hotten from North Dakota, and this man here is Munoz from Texas."

Just then, a commanding officer appeared in the doorway. "GET IN LINE, YOU MAGGOTS! WE'RE GOING TO DO SOMETHING ABOUT THAT HAIR!"

Lynn and the rest of the new recruits filed into a wide-open barbershop and stood in line for the shortest haircut of their lives. Tufts of loose hair were piling high on aproned shoulders and circling the floor around cushioned barber chairs. It was the 1980s, so most of the guys had a lot to lose. Shaggy heads walked in, and buzzed recruits walked out. The rest of the day encompassed more orientation, including physical training, and lasted late into the night. By the time Lynn reached his bunk, the exhaustion was bone-deep. He could see the same weariness reflected on the faces around him, and he knew they were just as tired as he was. Lynn hoped for a decent night's sleep, knowing it would start all over again the next day, but after what only felt like minutes, Lynn was jolted awake by garbage cans being thrown around the room.

"GET UP, YOU MUDDA PUCKERS!" Commander Garcia screamed. It was three-thirty in the morning and Lynn leaped out of bed, coming to attention alongside the rest of Company 927, but being drowsy and unfamiliar with their surroundings, most of the recruits stumbled around, trying to find their bearings.

"TWO MINUTES TO DRESS AND LINE UP! GO!"

Lynn feverishly threw his uniform on and lined up alongside the others. It was inoculation day but no one quite knew what that would mean. Filing in once more, Lynn felt like a member of a herd of cattle, preparing to be shot with vaccinations into his arm by an array of air guns. He nervously watched the men at the front of the line as the gun was pressed into the meat of their arms, just below the shoulder. They flinched as it fired a cocktail of vaccinations into the muscle. With each shot, the group shifted down the assembly line to the next attendant and the process was repeated. One recruit jumped as the air gun was fired, and the result was a stream of blood dripping down his arm.

Lynn approached the first attendant and watched as the man robotically gave him what felt like a punch to the arm. As he moved down the line, each inoculation was given in the same place, feeling like a boxing ring where the opponent has an obsession with hitting the same muscle until it's rendered useless. Lynn didn't know what specific vaccinations were in those cocktails, but he didn't want to ask. Once he and Neal returned to their barracks, they sunk into their bunks.

"That sucked!" Neal said, rubbing his arm.

"It's like they say, once you join the military, they own your body," Lynn replied.

Having to trade in his Alta shirt for a Naval uniform, Lynn was only beginning to leave his former self behind. Absolutely nothing could be kept and worn from home, including his deodorant and pair of glasses. Instead, they were replaced with Navy-regulated items, and Lynn was issued a pair of spectacles affectionately called "birth control glasses." When he sent home a picture of himself, smiling in his new attire and standing next to Neal in the barracks, Mickey stared in shock. With even less hair than he started with, some weight loss, and new glasses, Lynn was unrecognizable. Mickey pointed to Neal and said, "That's not Lynn, but I have no idea who this other guy is. What happened to my husband?!"

As both of them realized they would be making adjustments, Lynn focused on his training and realized the purpose of boot camp was to learn how to follow instructions. Every recruit was handed a cardboard stencil with punched-out letters and numbers for their last name, company number, last four digits of their social security number, and initials. They were instructed precisely where to place the stencil on each of their commissioned shirts and pants and how to paint on the markings. However, the blunders that were made were endless. Anyone who made a mistake was not allowed a set of replacement clothes even when the markings were made in several incorrect places on the same garment. The unfortunate recruits were forced to wear them anyway. Looking silly, their clothes might as well have said, "Loser."

STEEP TERRAIN

Following instructions also meant each bunk had to be made *perfectly*. Lynn quickly learned from the other recruits how to crawl under his bed and reach through the chicken wires to pull the fitted sheet to the center, making it perfectly tight on top. No one slept on their meticulously made beds because inspections were a risk at all times. Thus, six nights a week, Lynn and his bunkmates slept on the cold concrete with one pillow for comfort. On Thursdays, the night before laundry day, they could finally use their beds and get a much better night's sleep. That is, until three or four in the morning when Commander Garcia started his morning routine of cussing and throwing metal garbage cans.

The one benefit of being stationed at Coronado was the proximity to Lynn's favorite scuba diving destinations. Of course, he wasn't able to indulge in the fun during basic training, but he could smell the sea and was flooded with memories of dive trips he and his buddies had taken off the nearby coast. As Lynn settled in for another night on the hard floor, his mind drifted to one of his favorite trips where his old friend, a dive boat called *The Bottom Scratcher*, was docked at Point Loma. It was ten years before joining the Navy when Lynn and a small group of ski patrolmen were headed to the Channel Islands, including Lynn's scuba mentors, Linda and Garth Nelson, who owned the shop where Lynn learned to dive.

As they heaved their oxygen tanks, masks, and wet suits onto the deck, they chatted excitedly, eager to begin another trip. Lynn grabbed his bag and headed below to his cabin, looking forward to a good night's sleep before they would spend all day in the ocean. Waiting for their midnight departure, the group laughed and joked late into the night. The stars crept overhead, but only the brightest could compete with the glow of the nearby city lights. Soon, the boat's engine rumbled to life, and *The Bottom Scratcher* peeled away from the dock. They left the harbor behind, and Lynn fell into a deep sleep with the rolling of the ocean swells.

The next morning as he walked out on the deck, he saw the sun peeking over the horizon and knew they were almost there. Lynn inhaled the fresh, salty air, and felt refreshed after a busy week at MEPCO. However, he noticed his buddies were not feeling as chipper as he was and, instead, were leaning over the sides and heaving into the ocean.

"You guys have got to shake that seasickness someday," Lynn teased. "I'm hungry. Gonna get me some grub." He sauntered back below deck and headed for the galley where he noticed the cook wasn't fairing much better than his friends. Her skin was ghostly, and she clung to the counter in a struggle to hold her bearings. As the boat rolled with the sea, the eggs roamed over the sizzling stovetop. When she spotted Lynn, she bolted and ran topside to join the rest.

"I guess it's just me then," Lynn said and cooked the rest of breakfast himself.

As Lynn cleared off his plate of eggs, the boat dropped anchor just off San Clemente Island, and the group's morale rose significantly, knowing they'd finally get a break from the nausea. Not that Lynn needed the relief. His stomach was made of steel and figured nothing could crack it. After prepping their oxygen tanks, the group squeezed into their wetsuits since Pacific Coastal waters are cold enough to require protection, either a dry suit or a wet suit. Drysuits are like being strapped into a garbage bag, keeping you warm by preventing you from getting wet in the first place, while wet suits are the equivalent of squeezing into another layer of skin, except tighter. When the water is extra cold, a hood is worn, complete with a hearty dose of claustrophobia.

Despite the chilly waters, Lynn favored Southern California because of its unique sea life. Vast forests of kelp reaching over one-hundred-feet-tall sway with the current and give the sea a three-dimensional feel not often experienced on coral reefs. The water shades everything in a blue-green hue, and Lynn watched as two sea lions chased each other around like dogs, making a show of gliding along the surface and weaving through the kelp. They jetted around with impressive bursts of speed and lived up to their title as one of the most playful animals on the planet.

"Wow!" Lynn thought as he suddenly looked over his shoulder. A giant grouper coasted by like a camouflage-colored cruise ship. Lynn knew they were friendly, but they were still intimidating with a mouth large enough to swallow a grown man. He gazed at the ocean floor where a carpet of algae revealed little evidence of the rock beneath and where lobsters and crabs scurried here and there, duking it out with each other. There were sheep crabs that looked like angry rocks, and the small, red crabs could be easily mistaken for crawfish or jumbo shrimp. On each of these trips, Lynn and his buddies kept a pot of boiling water topside just for these occasions. Swimming down to the bottom, Lynn grabbed a lobster by the back of the shell and carried it topside. Only lobsters on the East Coast have massive claws, so there would be no risk of losing a finger. Lynn popped his fins off and climbed aboard, chucking the lobster into the pot. A few minutes later, he used a pair of tongs to pull it out, now flushed red, and cracked the shell to reveal buttery white meat that reminded him of his blissful days in the Blue Lagoon.

Lynn with a prized lobster

Jumping back into the water, Lynn followed Garth down to the sea bottom for another helping of tasty treats. Garth pulled out a knife and used the blade to scrape a scallop off a large rock. He swished it around in the water to rinse the sand off and then, pulling the regulator out of his mouth, popped the scallop in and ate it. Lynn was awestruck. "That is the manliest man I've ever met," he thought.

On an earlier trip, Lynn, Garth, and Linda had gone diving with Lynn's mother, Colleen, when things had taken a dangerous turn. Colleen was an inexperienced diver, and, even though she loved the colorful array of sea life, her anxiety caused her to breathe at an accelerated rate, using up her oxygen much faster than expected. Suddenly realizing she had run out of air at forty feet deep, she furiously gestured for help. Linda swam over but didn't have her emergency regulator with her, so she pulled her main regulator from her mouth and handed it to Colleen, saving her life. Colleen grabbed it and furiously sucked in a lungful of air, but, even as relief slowly crossed Colleen's face, Linda knew Lynn's mother would be too scared to give up the lifeline, and she would have to continue holding her breath. They would have to ascend slowly, taking care to prevent the deadly decompression sickness, or "the bends," by allowing their bodies to release the built-up nitrogen gas and avoid bubbles from developing in their bloodstream. At the time, the guideline was to ascend no faster than sixty feet per minute, so Linda patiently held her breath as she slowly guided Colleen the forty feet to the surface.

Back in the Channel Islands, Lynn was relaxing on the boat deck, taking a break between dives and letting his seafood feast digest. As he squinted into the horizon, he could see a group of people swimming far from land, but there was no boat nearby to aid them. Splashes surrounded them as they propelled themselves through the ocean swells, rising and falling with the sea. "Those guys have to be Navy SEALs," Lynn thought. "No one else would be that crazy."

"BOOM!" All at once, Lynn saw an explosion of sand fly skyward from the beach at San Clemente Island, a place that was strictly military and off-limits to civilians. He turned to find the artillery's origin and squinted into the horizon where a Naval Cruiser was stationed far out to sea. The artillery fired again, and Lynn heard a faint "Boom" in the distance. An artillery shell whizzed overhead, making a "Whoosh" and leaving a thin trail of smoke as it headed for the island.

"BOOM!" The beach erupted again, and another burst of sand shot skyward. Lynn didn't like the idea of sitting under the crossfire of a Naval Cruiser, and the captain of *The Bottom Scratcher* agreed.

"Let's move!" the captain said, and they high-tailed it out of there.

....

After waking from a half night's sleep back at boot camp, Lynn was assigned to the task of cleaning toilets with a toothbrush. He scrubbed for hours, carefully ensuring the glistening thrones would pass inspection when a tall, broad-chested recruit walked in. The man passed by the urinals and, much to Lynn's distress, peed in one of the toilets. The inevitable spray meant Lynn would have to start over, and the thought nearly made him lose all reason.

"Are you kidding me?!" Lynn called out. "Be thoughtful of your classmates here. Someone has to clean that up!"

"I'm sorry!" the man backpedaled and quickly left the bathroom.

Lynn couldn't believe he had lost his temper at someone who could easily have squashed him like a roach. He remained emphatically grateful the man was kind enough not to retaliate. Despite the pressures all the recruits undergo during basic training, Lynn found the most challenging part was being away from Mickey, who was now pregnant with twins. In the back of his mind, he also maintained an irrational fear of never returning to civilian life. There was a place on the base where he could look down and see a gas station, a place where people could fill up their tanks and go wherever they wanted. "If only I could do that," he thought. Lynn noticed one of the recruits was always smiling and was perplexed at how the man could maintain such a sunny disposition. "I've already been through Army boot camp," the man said. "This is nothing."

The worst day of training arrived. Lynn and the rest of Company 927 were headed to the gas chamber, affectionately nicknamed the "confidence chamber." Lynn was handed a gas mask, instructed on how to properly put it on, and then herded into an airtight room. The company donned their masks and heard the doors seal shut behind them. Once the tear gas was released, Lynn and every other recruit were required to remove their mask and repeat a phrase specifically chosen to force them into taking a breath, often a portion of "The Star-Spangled Banner." As soon as Lynn finished his phrase and took a gasp of air, a full assault on his senses hit him like a train. Tears and snot poured from his face as he coughed and sputtered while several other students vomited all over the concrete floor. Once every mask was off and the last recruit had finished speaking their phrase, the doors opened, and Lynn was released into a merciful lungful of fresh air. The burning sensation persisted, but he began to feel some relief as the minutes rolled on. He watched a crew take a hose and sprayed the vomit off the chamber's floor, readying it for the next wave of recruits.

Lynn was at an advantage when it came time to handle a rifle, having spent his youth deer hunting with his dad. Don had given him a Mauser bolt-action rifle, a token of their German ancestry, and the two made good use of it on the local populations of white-tailed deer. The more challenging task for Lynn was learning how to disassemble and re-assemble it, and quickly, but he kept up with his classmates and performed well. Since small arms combat is rare in the open ocean, Lynn found the firearms training in the Navy to be minimal in comparison to other branches of the military. The next segment of their training promised to be more useful.

It was swim day, and the commanding officer gathered the men poolside. Everyone was expected to get wet; it was the Navy after all, but one young man hesitated.

"WHAT IS YOUR PROBLEM, SAILOR?!"

"I don't know how to swim, sir. The recruiter promised the Navy would teach me."

"YOU DON'T KNOW HOW TO SWIM? HOW DO YOU EXPECT TO BE A PROPER SAILOR IF YOU CAN'T SWIM? GET IN THE WATER WITH THE REST OF THE RECRUITS!"

The reluctant student was forced into the deep end of the pool, and the officer took a long rescue pole off the wall and used it to push him into the middle and keep him there so he couldn't reach the sides. The young man struggled and gasped but eventually learned. "I guess the recruiter was right," Lynn thought. A few days later, everyone was outside when a recruit from Montana fell to the deck, holding his gut and groaning. Lynn ran to his side and began to assess him. As the officer on deck arrived, Lynn identified himself. "I am medically trained, sir! This man is suffering from a distended bowel."

"YOU ARE A RECRUIT, NOTHING MORE! NOW, GET AWAY FROM THAT STUDENT!"

"Yes, sir! Please transport him quickly."

The group dispersed, and, as Lynn made his way back to the barracks, Neal slapped him on the back and said, "You're a natural physician, Falkner."

After graduating from basic training, Lynn immediately jumped into Hospital Corpsman A School. Even though he was looking forward to getting home and being with Mickey, he thrived in the academic environment and was glad to be back in medicine. He knew he would need help getting accepted into the PA program and had been told corpsmen with experience in the Vietnam war had been given high priority. Nothing beats the kind of hands-on experience war can give a medic, but Vietnam was before Lynn's time, so he had to hope the credentials would give him a boost anyway.

During those fourteen weeks in school, he prioritized his studies and worked hard. It paid off when his exam scores came back, and Lynn realized he had obtained the highest score in Naval history. An admiral asked to interview him, hoping to put the achievement on the front page of a Naval magazine, but the plan quickly unraveled when she asked him what had motivated him to work so hard. "I just want to get out of here," he replied. The article was dropped to a small blurb in the back.

14

Steel Armadillo

"I sure hope we can get a good deal for this clunker so we can come home without it," Lynn said, having just returned from San Diego. "Let's take separate cars, in case we get lucky."

"Amen to that," Mickey said, showing every bit of her eight-month pregnancy with twins as she wedged herself into their other car. "I'm grateful we're finally both out of school. We've earned an upgrade."

"At least something more reliable, that's for sure."

Lynn climbed into his eighteen-year-old '64 Chevy Impala, and they each pulled out of the driveway. As they headed down State Street, they began looking for a used car lot that might take their geriatric beater. Lynn spotted a Toyota dealership with a sign on the curb that read, "We pay cash for used cars," and pulled in.

"Looking to sell?" the dealer asked.

"Yep."

"Well, let's take it for a spin."

Mickey waited in her car while Lynn and the dealer puttered around the parking lot in the Impala. It was blowing too much smoke to keep its meager worth a secret, but Lynn and Mickey still hoped for a fair deal to put towards a newer vehicle. After returning, Lynn and the dealer walked inside and got down to brass tacks.

"What would you give me for it?" Lynn asked.

The dealer stared at him for a moment and said, "You look like a gamblin' man. It's only worth about $200, but, if we flip, I'll give you double. What do you say, double or nothing?"

Lynn thought for a minute. "Let's do it."

The dealer pulled a coin from his pocket and flicked it into the air. He caught it and smacked it onto the back of his hand, lifting his palm for the reveal. As Lynn saw the coin, his heart stopped. A few minutes later, he walked outside to see Mickey.

"How much did you get for it?"

"Nothing," he admitted.

"WHAT?! Why? How?"

"The man offered me double if I'd flip for it," he said. She was dumbfounded.

Despite some fallout after giving their car away, Lynn was ecstatic to be back home. From then on, he only spent two weeks each year in San Diego, plus one weekend a month at the military base back home. Like most corpsmen, Lynn was assigned to a Marine battalion and worked at the Army base for their weekend duties. He would arrive early in the morning, climb into an eight-wheeled, windowless armored personnel vehicle, and tuck himself into the back. These transports were amphibious and had small, caged propellers stuck to the back. Sitting in the middle of the desert, the propellers looked less like something on a boat and more like fans mounted to help the Marines stay cool during the blazing heat of an afternoon. The vehicle looked like a tank if you removed the gun turret and poked a straw inside to puff it up like a balloon. With eight beefy tires, it sat low to the ground, and one of the Marines had the job of wiggling underneath to inspect the belly every time it stopped. Lynn sat in the darkness all weekend as Marines came and went, hour after hour, motoring around in the steel armadillo.

When it was time to apply for PA school, Lynn was discouraged to learn his experience as a corpsman wouldn't help get him through the acceptance process as he had hoped. However, his record-setting Naval exams did. It was an elating moment, but, with a new career on the horizon and newborn twin daughters, he knew changes needed to be made. He had spent twenty years at Alta, and now it was time to hang up his patrol jacket for good. Several of his ski buddies had moved on as well, some attended medical school and becoming M.D.s, one returned to his family's cattle ranch, and another become our family's dentist. However, there were a few who never left and who continued to live the snow-covered dream.

Physician Assistant school started with Lynn's nose in a book. It was like drinking from a firehose, but he thrived in it. He barely left the classroom the first year, but his second brought field training where he visited clinics and watched providers work. The most unexpected challenge was realizing when he couldn't take his patients at their word because their stories sometimes contradicted the evidence. Lynn's first rotation was in a nursing home where he was asked to interview a resident and give a brief examination. He paired up with a lady sitting in a cushy armchair and began asking some routine medical history questions. Noticing her mysteriously swollen abdomen, he asked, "Ma'am, I'm wondering why your belly is so distended. Do you drink alcohol?"

"Nah, I never touched the stuff."

He suspected a case of ascites, a condition caused by heavy drinking, but, with her confident denial, he crossed it off the list. He finished the exam and waited for the report to be reviewed.

"What do you mean it's not ascites?" his instructor replied. "She had her own still!"

Lynn had already taken an Advanced Trauma Life Support (ATLS) course in the Navy and was ready to repeat it in PA school. ATLS courses focus on assessing a patient's condition and providing immediate management to an injury. Lynn and his classmates practiced on goats, but always with a veterinarian standing by to make sure the animals didn't suffer. Lynn practiced inserting IVs and performing tracheotomies, a method of inserting a tube into the airway to help a patient breathe. The instructors also brought in a bunch of pig's feet, since they are considered the closest to human skin and therefore the perfect material to practice on. The instructors cut lacerations into the skin of the pig's feet, and then hand one to each of the students to suture up.

The workload was a full-time job, and the instructors emphasized prioritizing their studies over anything else. Most students put families and jobs on hold until they graduated, but Lynn already had twins at home and began looking for a part-time job to help cover the bills.

"There's an opening for an anesthesiology technician at the children's hospital," Mickey said. "You should take it."

"How am I supposed to perform a job I can't even spell?"

"Come on, give it a try," she said and gave him a nudge. He took the job.

Lynn had planned to use his career as a PA to move with Mickey to a rustic Montana area like Flathead Lake and care for the community there. After all, the profession of a PA was created to bring doctors to rural communities with the program accepting students in the hopes they would return to their small hometowns and set up family practices there. However, those well-laid plans would change the day Lynn met Dr. Marion "Jack" Walker.

Mickey was already working at Primary Children's Medical Center as an x-ray technician and knew most of the staff, so she introduced Lynn to Dr. Walker, the big cheese of Primary's pediatric neurosurgery department. He was a kind and gentle man, well suited for the position, and a stark contrast to the egotistical personalities the profession often magnetizes. As Lynn neared graduation, Mickey turned to Jack and said, "I think you need a PA."

"Our department has never had a PA before," he said. "There will be hoops to jump through and red tape to cut. I agree with you, though. I'll try and make it happen."

Several board meetings were held, and by-laws were changed. The big wigs finally approached Lynn and said, "You can do all the procedures you've requested, but you can't close dura in the ER."

"That won't be a problem," Lynn said since he knew no one closes the lining around the brain in an ER anyway.

"You also can't re-attach tendons."

"Okay, I can live with that," Lynn said. He wouldn't need to worry about that either, since one touches tendons in neurosurgery. They gave him the job, and Lynn began working directly for Jack Walker. As a fresh PA school graduate, Lynn had the same feeling he had as a newly minted pilot; he now had a license to begin learning. "Looking back, even I wouldn't have flown with me. Too risky," he said.

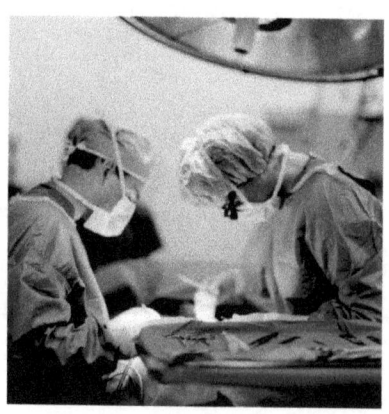

Lynn during surgery

Lynn worked with everything on and around the brain, including blood clots, major bleeding, and the opening and closing of the skull. However, if the procedure involved going inside the brain, Lynn stayed out. He was also frequently asked to be the liaison between the department and the patients' families since his kind and personable nature instilled comfort amid the serious diseases and injuries they were navigating. Much like Jack, he was compassionate, gentle, and helped parents and patients understand their situation without the confusion of medical jargon.

On one occasion, Lynn was called into the operating room where a young girl needed a blood clot removed from her brain. After scrubbing in, his first task was to remove a section of her skull, a procedure called a craniotomy. To reach the bone, he took a scalpel and carefully cut a line around her ear and then up and over her head to the other ear. Keeping the incision above her hairline allowed him to hide any future scarring, especially since facial skin is notorious for scarring heavily. He gently pulled the skin down to her eyebrows and draped it gently over her nose.

Next, he grabbed the craniotome, a metal drill resembling a hot glue gun or chef's blow torch for a crème brulée. Power tools used in hospital operating rooms are almost identical to the ones found at Lowes or Home Depot and are either electric or powered by compressed air, called pneumatic. Lynn pressed the craniotome to the exposed skull and squeezed the trigger. As it made a "Zzoot, Zzoot" sound, it drilled a burr hole into the bone, and the pressure-sensitive safety mechanism shut the drill off as soon as he broke through. Whenever Lynn needed to remove the skull of a new baby, the bone was soft enough not to need a drill at all. Instead, Lynn used scissors and snipped through as if working on a grade school art project.

Sometimes when the brain needs a little pressure relief, such as from fluid buildup, burr holes are all that's needed; however, this little girl had a blood clot underneath the skull that needed to be scraped out. Lynn grabbed a different pneumatic tool, this one called the Midas Rex, and followed the burr holes like a connect-the-dots picture, cutting a large, round section of the bone from her head. There, pressed into her brain, was a two-inch-thick blood clot. He scraped it out, bit by bit, and then carefully replaced the segment of bone as if he was putting the top back on a Jack-o-Lantern that had just been gutted.

When the brain undergoes significant trauma, the swelling can prevent the bone from being replaced right away, and is, instead, left out until the swelling subsides, usually for a week or two. Trying to put the bone back amidst serious swelling is like trying to stuff a Christmas tree back in the original box, and there's only a tiny amount of stuffing a surgeon can perform safely. Excessive swelling requires the wound to be closed up without the bone, and during that time the bone is kept in the patient's belly, between the fat and muscle tissue. It's a safe place where it can remain healthy, and the hospital doesn't need to worry about it getting lost in a freezer. When it's time to return it, the surgeons remove it from the patient's belly and put it back in their head. It's a bizarre sight to see someone missing a piece of their skull after the swelling has gone down because it leaves a big divot in their head.

Speaking of something from a science fiction movie, halos are also a sight to behold, although they're commonly depicted in medical dramas. While Lynn was making his rounds one morning to check on all the neurosurgery patients, he walked into the room of a young boy injured in a car accident. The boy was sitting upright against the back of his bed and was working on a cup of chocolate pudding. Lynn greeted him and carefully inspected the circular rim of metal wrapped around his head with a couple of inches of space between it and the skin, looking like the namesake would suggest. It was screwed directly into the boy's skull with bolts around his head and then secured his neck in a fixed position by four long rods that reached a vest strapped to his chest.

Although halos are common in practice, Lynn heard a valid argument against their use to stabilize neck injuries. A man named Dr. James Bailey told him, "Try grabbing a snake at the head and the tail and act like a rigid halo. Look at how much movement a snake still has in the middle, writhing around. Even if the top and the bottom hold, the middle can still move." Halos take a lot of effort to surgically install, so doctors want to make sure they have benefit. Another common use is to hold a patient's head perfectly still for a set of MRI scans so doctors can document landmarks, minimizing the risk of mistakes. "That's a great purpose for a halo," Lynn said.

On a routine pop-in to say hello to Mickey, Lynn took a stroll down to the CT department and waited for her in the control room while she finished with a kid on the scanning bed. He patiently watched her through the large viewing window when the child suddenly projectile vomited all over her. She was completely covered. It was a head injury-level vomiting session and left a clean shadow on the wall where Mickey was standing. She gestured desperately to Lynn, "Get in here and get some towels!" but he could only stand there with his mouth hanging open and an expression that said, "No way." Lynn didn't handle vomit well, so Mickey watched in disbelief as he gathered some towels and chucked them into the scanning room before doing a quick swivel and high-tailing it out the door. She was left alone with the child, who was also covered in puke, but was able to swiftly rally some help from a nearby department. Lynn may have escaped the vomit, but he knew he wouldn't escape the wrath that would be waiting for him at home.

15

Bouncy Houses

Being a Physician Assistant in a neurosurgery department was like working as a permanent resident doctor, a bottom-of-the-totem-pole member of the surgical team who worked exceptionally long hours. Lynn was averaging 120-hour weeks and performing much of the same duties, rarely having the chance to visit home or sleep in his own bed. Not everyone in the office carried such a heavy load, and it was before medical reforms would restrict the number of hours a doctor could work. During weekend shifts, Lynn was on duty from Friday morning until Monday night. Awake. On the rare occasion he could lie on a cot tucked away in his windowless office, he'd be out like a light, but it was never long before the next call came in. Some of the calls were trivial and took every morsel of his willpower not to shout, "You can't call me for this! Just let me sleep!"

At the top of the hierarchy was the attending physician, Dr. Jack Walker; then a "fellow," who was a doctor finished with training but learning a specialty; and then at the bottom was Lynn, alongside the neurosurgery residents. "He became an integral part of the department and helped train the residents. Somehow, he managed not to be intimidating to them," Jack said. "That in itself speaks to his great interpersonal skills," he continued. It would be several years before Lynn could reduce his hours and spend more time at home, but to make up for his absence, he brought home trays full of cafeteria food to my mother, Alyssa, and me. Thirty years later, two of those trays are still sitting on my parents' fridge, and are used every time they need help carrying hot dogs and the fixin's out to the grill. The old children's hospital where they came from has since been demolished; otherwise, they probably would have sent my dad a bill.

With my dad practically living at the hospital and my mother also working there full-time, Alyssa and I spent the first five years of our lives with a nanny named Penny Loback. She was as much of a grandmother to us as our real ones were and loved us as her own. Our mother still cared for us in the evenings and tucked us in each night, and our dad snuck away from work on his lunch breaks to squeeze us with hugs. If he made it home at night, he would sneak into our rooms to kiss us goodnight no matter how late it was. Even though I know my parents wanted to spend more time with us, they did the right thing. I'm grateful they dedicated themselves to the young patients who needed them more than Alyssa and I did at the time, thanks to Penny.

When Penny had grandchildren of her own, we lost her as our nanny, but not before we had developed a life-long bond or before she could record herself reading our favorite books. We continued to visit her, her children, and her grandchildren like any other members of our family, celebrating adoptions, weddings, birthdays, or for no occasion at all. When she finally passed away, my mom was holding her hand.

While Penny had been tending her own grandchildren, Alyssa and I bounced around with a few other nannies, but nothing stuck. Eventually, we attended afterschool programs and day camps during the summer. I often felt isolated from my parents, but I don't regret a single moment because I know those children needed them, and I am grateful to have been able to sacrifice in my own small way.

There are many ways my upbringing has affected the way I parent, but it's not always conscious. After my two eldest daughters completed their first two years of school, I pulled them and began homeschooling. It had many benefits, but my overarching concern was not feeling like a mom because I never saw my kids. In the state where we were living, public school was an all-or-nothing deal. Even for kids as young as three, they were gone nine hours a day, plus an hour of homework, and then bedtime directly after. I felt my children barely knew me and had no time to scrape their knees and have a normal childhood.

We homeschooled for four wonderful years, but since then, my daughters have returned to public school. I now have a third daughter who attends a Pre-Kindergarten class, but I am protective of her needs. Whenever she feels overwhelmed or exhausted and needs time to be at home, I let her, the state requirements be damned.

My parent's service-driven mindset was apparent in more than just their career fields. As my sister and I were growing up, they took us to police and fire stations every Christmas to drop off boxes of chocolates or homemade cookies. I have happily passed on that tradition, including finding other ways to involve my children in service opportunities. I may not have a career in medicine as they did, but I have been attempting to teach my children the importance of making the world a better place, one day at a time. I realized something must have stuck when my seven-year-old daughter, Claire, asked to take her silk flowers from her birthday party to our modest, rural cemetery and replace the tattered, sun-bleached ones. As she arranged the flowers, we read the gravestones and talked about the children buried there. One of the graves had a marker of hand-poured concrete and it appeared the family had used a stick to carve in the name of their own seven-year-old daughter.

When my dad's work hours kept him at the hospital around the clock, the old facility was closed down, and a new one was built. This newly minted Primary Children's Hospital was designed specifically for children, right down to the windows, which were jumbo-sized and reached low enough for even the smallest children to gaze through. The picturesque scene of snow-capped mountains could be viewed on one side, and the Great Salt Lake lined the horizon on the other. Hallways were lined with colorful drawings of ladybugs, dinosaurs, and stick figures made by children of every age. The rooms felt bright, and many were decorated with decals of cute cartoon animals. Even the MRI machine sported decals of palm trees with hanging bananas and monkeys. I frequently begged my dad to bring some home for my bedroom walls, and a couple of times, he granted my wish. Those cartoon lobsters and clownfish made me feel like

I could see the ocean reefs from his adventures, which he had told me about so many times.

The food at the hospital was another category altogether. There was no skimping on quality, and dishes were served twenty-four hours a day. Buttery salmon, hot green bean casserole, and sweet blueberry pie were just a few items on an ever-changing menu, and my dad admitted he gained a few pounds because of it. It was even rated a four-star restaurant on Yelp.com, and the staff at neighboring hospitals would sneak to Primary just for a plate.

On the morning rounds, Lynn and a couple of other department members of neurosurgery made the mistake of walking into "King's X," a large room full of activities and toys where no doctors were allowed for any reason, even to talk with their patients. It was created to give the kids a place to feel safe, and where friendly staff would help them glue crafts together and cut things up. As Lynn and the team approached in their white lab coats, the staff quickly blocked the path and kicked them out. "You're not allowed in here. It's forbidden!"

The Newborn Intensive Care Unit, or NICU, had a less official King's X policy. Despite the neurosurgery team having full access to the area, the NICU staff felt protective of their tiny cherubs. When Lynn and the team approached for a welfare check, one of the neonatology doctors stood in their way, and raised his arms like Moses, saying, "Everybody get prepared! Neurosurgery is here!"

Both Lynn and Mickey were an excellent fit for Primary, dedicating themselves to helping any child who passed through.

Opportunities to cheer up homesick kids were always in demand, and they jumped at every occasion. On Halloween, Mickey wore a giant plastic butt under a hospital gown that never ceased to draw snickers and giggles. Since the gowns tie in the back and never hide everything, both the kids and adults loved laughing at her oversized and "naked" butt.

Alyssa and I were often brought in while our parents worked, usually on Saturday mornings, and were treated as honorary members of Primary's Imaging Department. Our mother would ask for help "warming up the CT machine," which meant we could lay on the scanning bed and watch cartoons while she readied it for the first patient of the day. The bed was hard and extremely narrow, only wide enough to fit our small shoulders, so we had to lay end to end. My mom would grab two white hospital blankets and tuck us in, warm and cozy, before slipping in a movie and disappearing into the dark control room.

The MRI machine was a whole different animal. While it was warming up, it had a similar hum to the CT scanner, but, when it was taking images, it sounded like a broken washing machine. "Clunk. Bang. Clunk. Clunk. Bang." I could never find a pattern, and only heard random clunking and banging. I wondered how something so technologically advanced could sound like something pulled from an old yard sale. However, the best part about the MRI was when our mom let us "walk the wool."

After a quick inspection for metal in my pockets, she gave me a ball of steel wool tied with some string as a leash. Clutching the wool, I crossed the marked threshold into the MRI room and placed the ball at the end of the narrow scanning bed. I led the wool along like a pet out for a stroll and inched ever closer to the mouth of the machine. As my proximity narrowed, the magnetic charge coming from the dark tunnel gave the wool an energy of its own. It slid ahead of my hand and began pulling me instead. The closer we got, the harder it pulled, until finally it lifted off the bed and suspended itself in the air, like a kite. Just as I reached the gaping tunnel, the wool was pulling hard enough that I worried it would rip from my hand and go sailing deep inside. I don't remember my mother telling me there would be consequences if that happened, but I felt like there would be, so I made sure to never let go.

Spending time in my dad's office was a completely different adventure. The neurosurgery department had a hallway lined with small offices, but Alyssa and I knew the best place to play was with the copy machine. It was kept in a small, windowless, filing room where we enjoyed the absence of prying eyes from suspicious adults. We copied everything we could find, usually our faces and hands, but sometimes a toy or two. Then one day, we came up with the best idea of all—our butts. We made sure the door was fully closed and no one was around before pulling down our pants and taking turns sitting on the glass, pressing our little cheeks in all their glory. When we proudly presented the art to our dad, he rushed to hide them under his lab coat and told us we couldn't do it anymore. I'm sure he burned those papers the first chance he got. I can't imagine how much paper we used with that machine, but it probably took out half the Amazon.

One day while concocting strange potions with the break room soda fountain, I decided to play in the department's play area, a place where we spent a surprisingly little amount of time.

I began playing with a plastic T-Rex that had an open mouth, which led to a big, hollow belly. When I tipped it forward to help it "eat" another toy, out poured a pool of rotten, curdled milk. I don't think I've ever seen milk that far gone, before or since. I guess some kid thought the T-Rex had been thirsty and decided to share some of their moo juice.

I never recognized how different Primary was from traditional hospitals until my dad took me to visit my grandmother, Colleen, at the neighboring hospital where she now worked as a nurse. The dark hallways were lined in red brick and were bare of any artwork. It was a stark contrast to what I was accustomed to, and it lived up to the gloomy atmosphere children usually associate with hospitals.

Walking down the hallways of Primary behind our dad, we often ended up in the Intensive Care Unit, or ICU. If a patient was there, it meant they were in especially bad shape. Before pushing through the swinging doors, my dad would turn to us for a reminder.

"Girls, remember to be quiet and stick close to me."

"Okay," we chimed together.

As the doors swung open, we saw bed after bed of kids barely visible under tubes, blankets, and bandages. Each child was surrounded by machines, monitoring vitals, feeding IV fluids, and pumping air into their lungs. As we walked, my dad nodded his head to one of the patients and said, "That kid wasn't wearing a seat belt." My sister and I cowered. Nodding towards another, he said, "That kid wasn't wearing a helmet while riding his bike." Our eyes grew wider as we contemplated the sobering consequences. It wasn't until years later that he confessed he was making it up. Even though he had seen countless injuries resulting from kids not wearing helmets or seatbelts, he was not assigned to these particular patients and had no idea what caused their hospital stay. It was a scare tactic meant to keep us as safe as possible. He had seen enough tragedy over the years and didn't want us to become a part of it. In fact, one of the worst cases he ever saw was the result of a bouncy house.

Bouncy houses get a bad rap for the bruises and bloody noses they can cause, even catching kids' braces in their webbing, but for a seven-year-old girl, the damage was far more severe. Unfortunately, she was playing in one that had not been securely staked to the ground, and it got swept up by a gust of wind, carrying it through the air like a sail with her still in it. It flew up high, flipped over, and came crashing down on its top. The air-filled cushion padded the bottom, but the top was just a sheet of plastic, offering no protection whatsoever. She landed on her face, and everything from her ears forward was shattered: her forehead, nose, sinuses, jaw, and teeth. Even her orbits, the bone sockets where eyes are kept, were crushed, and one of her eyes was hanging out. "She underwent many surgeries," my dad said, "but she still didn't look normal. It must have been pretty rough. One minute she's having fun in a bouncy house, and the next she's a star pupil at Primary Children's."

16

What Hump?

"Lynn, I'd like you to check in our visiting surgeon," Jack said. "He's from Brazil and will be here for three months fulfilling his pediatric training. I want you to watch over him for me. His name's Humberto de Aquino."

"Absolutely," Lynn said half-heartedly. He enjoyed the rotating doctors but was feeling overworked and didn't think he had time to be a tour guide. After avoiding Humberto for three days, the two found themselves standing in the department break room together.

"Lynn, what it mean, 'Way to go?'" Humberto asked.

"Humberto, if you make a soccer goal and score, it's 'Way to go, Humberto,' but if you try to score the goal and miss, it's also 'Way to go, Humberto.'" Lynn left him in a state of complete confusion, but from then on, they were bonded.

My dad invited him to our family's home often, where he shared with us his Brazilian culture and strummed my mother's guitar. The steel strings were not to his liking, so my dad took him downtown to Acoustic House, a small music store repurposed from an old bungalow and displaying beautiful guitars from floor to ceiling. Humberto carefully pulled one down, quietly tuned the strings, and began playing the smooth, rhythmic cords of Bossa Nova. Everyone in the shop stopped and listened. As he sat wrapped in the melody, a fellow musician tapped him on the shoulder.

"Where did you learn such incredible Brazilian music?" the man asked. Without lifting his eyes or missing a chord, Humberto tipped his head in the man's direction and said, "Brazil." He brought home a pair of gut strings that turned my mother's guitar into a completely different instrument.

When Humberto had completed his three months of training, he flew back home but soon returned for a visit with his wife, Maria. My mother's guitar was restrung with the gut strings, and he gracefully strummed while singing beautiful duets with Maria, their favorite being "The Girl from Ipanema." Soon two daughters were born, and they were eventually brought to the States to meet us. As we chatted in my parent's living room, Humberto motioned for his six-year-old to come closer. He gently dipped her head and, across the back of her neck, used his finger to trace something as if he was reading it. He said, "Made in U.S.A."

When I was a teenager, my parents flew to Brazil to visit Humberto and Maria on their own turf. Humberto ran them ragged, proudly showing off his home country and helping them feast on Brazilian barbeque. After only a few hours of rest the first night, Humberto asked them if they had slept well. "Yes, Humberto, thank you," my dad said. To which he replied, "Good. No more sleep for you." When the eldest daughter, Barbara, entered high school, she moved in with us as a foreign exchange student and became a bridesmaid at my wedding. As I write this, the youngest daughter, Deborah, has completed her college degree and is flying up to live with my parents to gain work experience in the United States.

Another member of the resident surgical team was a born-and-raised Texan who claimed to have a god to protect them and their patients from the Four Horsemen of the Apocalypse. In a backroom behind the OR, he kept a shrine to this "protector," which consisted of a table set with salt, a lemon, and a shot of Tequila. Even though no one ever drank the Tequila, they got in trouble because it was actual liquor.

Operating rooms were a place of fast-paced, life-saving procedures, but also housed repetitive, low-risk ones as well. Lynn and the rest of the team wanted to break up the monotony during a routine surgery, so they slipped *Young Frankenstein* into a video player. ORs are full of fancy video equipment which helps surgeons view the intricacies of delicate blood vessels and nerves, while also minimizing the invasiveness of a procedure. Since audio would be unnecessary when using it for an operation, the flat screens didn't have speakers, but the team was happy to fill in the dialogue because they knew the lines by heart.

"We can take care of that hump," offered Dr. Frankenstein to Igor.

"What hump?" Igor asked. Not Egor; it was Igor. My dad will probably go to his grave quoting that movie. On a separate afternoon, the team noticed the lecture hall was empty, a place usually reserved for discussing medical cases, so the team took over the amphitheater and turned on *Unforgiven*, starring Clint Eastwood.

When it came time to put Alyssa and me in school, my dad asked around the hospital to find out where everyone else was sending their kids. Children of the brain and cardiovascular surgeons attended Roland Hall, the Catholic private school, but with such a heavy price tag, we were, instead, enrolled at the Jewish Community Center, a small school held in a synagogue and only hosted one class per grade. Surprisingly, the Jewish kids were the minority, and the principal was a Catholic named Dr. Debra Mohrman, pronounced "Mormon." Without a playground, my classmates and I created our own town and economy using the hills, rocks, and crab apple trees instead. My dad attended our class as a guest speaker on several occasions, bringing cow eyeballs, brains, and other organs for us to touch and feel. He loved children, and part of that joy came from making us squeal and shriek with tales of medical gore, all while handing us slimy, squishy organs. My sister and I thought we had the coolest dad on the planet, and the day he brought Humberto was even better.

On a field trip to Primary Children's, our second-grade class was listening to a nutritionist explain the food pyramid. He described what our bodies needed and what they didn't, saying, "Fats are just out." Hesitantly, a little hand rose into the air, and a young boy asked, "What about myelination of the brain?" Stunned silence settled over the room as the nutritionist tried to find the right words, and the rest of us were wondering what on Earth the kid was talking about.

I asked my dad, later, to explain myelination to me and he said, "It's the process that transforms the brain from a consistency of toothpaste that we have at birth to the firm organ we have in adulthood." He looked at the box fan on the floor and continued, "It's like the rubber coating around that electrical cord, and it's essential for brain function. As it develops, with the help of fats from our diet, it strengthens and solidifies. More than just helping our brains progress physically, it impacts cognitive function and coordination. It's the difference between a kid who can learn to ride a bike at two years old and a kid who learns at four. Complete myelination doesn't take place until after the age of twenty-one, years after gaining the right to vote." The boy was right, but the nutritionist was attempting to teach the unhealthiness of junk food like Twinkies and chips, while the boy was speaking of the healthy fats, which are necessary for developing brains, such as from milk and avocados. My impressive classmate was pulled from school that day and sent somewhere better suited to challenge his intellect.

While Lynn advanced his training, Jack Walker took him to an educational lab in Indiana, where they specialized in a very narrow set of procedures. Lynn's first task was to pick his subject from a big bin of real human heads. "It was eerie staring into their faces," he told me, "But it's better to practice drilling a hole into someone's skull when they're already dead." There was also a bin full of arms where a different group of students practiced endoscopic carpal tunnel repairs.

Lynn sat at a long table, staring into the face of his chosen subject. A plastic cube was placed around his workspace to protect the room from an inevitable spray of bodily fluids. Upon the subject's death, the heads had been removed, and a sealant spread over the neck to keep the fluids in the brain. Jack circled the room as he watched Lynn and several other students learn to pass a catheter from the brain to the base of the neck. When they had finished and were ready to move on, another instructor stepped up.

"I want you to perform a craniotomy using the Midas Rex," he called out. "As soon as you can show us you are capable with the Midas, we will sign your certificate, and you'll be permitted to use it in surgery."

The instructor walked over, and Lynn drilled a smooth hole through the bone, "Zzzuuut. Zzzuuut."

"I can tell you've done this before," he said. "You're not supposed to be using this tool without certification."

"Oops," Lynn thought.

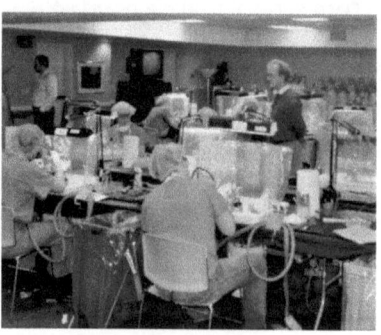

The lab in Indiana

Back in Salt Lake City, Lynn was tasked with a research project with the University of Utah where he helped test treatment methods for brain infections in children. Since rabbits have similar physiology to humans, several jumbo-sized bunnies took center stage. The team had high hopes, but, before they could make progress on the operating table, the anesthesia kept killing them. The project was shut down.

While on call one day, Lynn heard the medical helicopter was heading out and in need of a member of the neurosurgery team. It would be a trip to "Dinosaurland," the nickname given to a small, fossil-filled town 150 miles away called Vernal, Utah. It was Lynn's first time on the helicopter, and he was happy to see a familiar face on board, recognizing the flight nurse as a friend of his. As they lifted off the helipad on Primary's rooftop, the chopper beelined it for the rugged Wasatch Mountains. Instead of climbing to a high altitude, the pilot stayed low and followed the movement of the land, rising and falling with the shape of the canyons. Despite Lynn's stomach of steel, he worried the ups and downs would make the other passengers lose their last meals.

"Why don't we climb up to smoother air where we can fly straighter?" he asked.

"I'm a helicopter pilot. I get nosebleeds up there. Besides, I'm looking for elk."

After picking up the injured boy and beginning their return flight, Lynn watched the onboard nurse's extraordinary ability to insert an IV needle amidst the constant jostling of the helicopter, especially while everyone else was gripping the sides just to hang on.

"How can you do that?" he asked.

"I can only do it with the motion of flight. I can't do it on the ground," she said.

Apart from Lynn's time at Primary, he also fulfilled his yearly duties for the Navy, often being sent north to the Naval base in Bremerton, Washington, a shipyard made atomic submarines. When the next US president was elected, the vessels were ordered to be dismantled, leaving the workers who built them devastated. They had poured years of sweat and pride into the subs but were now required to take them apart, piece by piece. Fights would often break out in the shipyard, and sometimes a wrench would "accidentally" be dropped on someone's head. As the medical professional on duty, Lynn had his hands full.

One of his patients was a Marine who had been reprimanded for having too much nose hair and had attempted to fix it by taking a lighter and burning the insides of his nostrils. Lynn enjoyed serving the sailors on the West Coast, especially at the Naval Hospital where they had a tradition of feeding their people well, even offering lobster and generous portions of prime rib. When the facility was eventually torn down and Lynn was moved to the new one, Lynn had to be watchful not to bump into the robots that rolled down the hallways, delivering medicine to the patients.

When the Gulf War erupted and Operation Desert Storm began, my dad was placed on active duty and called to work full time in San Francisco. With the active military now in Iraq and the previous MD's working on the hospital ship, Mercy, Lynn held down the fort stateside. He ran a clinic on Treasure Island which resembled a family practice, treating both sailors and their families. During his six-month post there, it quickly became his favorite assignment of his Naval career,. My mother, Alyssa, and

I occasionally came to visit, enjoying the local zoo and parks while he patched up more sailors.

17

The Dangers of Being a Kid

At our dinner table, weird medical cases were my favorite topic. The infinite number of ways kids can get themselves into trouble, and the things they stick up their noses, never ceased to amaze me, even to this day. One evening while eating our typical meal of Hamburger Helper, my dad described a mother who had brought her son to see him, saying the boy's breath smelled so bad none of the other kids would play with him. Already suspicious of the cause, my dad noticed discharge coming from his nose, so he took a hemostat and reached up the boy's nostril. Out came what doctors refer to as a "foreign object," and my dad held it out for the mother to see. It was a tiny kickstand off a model motorcycle. It stunk to high heaven, but the kid was fine after that.

With my eyes wide with interest, my dad told me of another case which involved a kid falling on his family's TV antennae, back when TVs had "rabbit ears." The antennae had gone through the corner of his eye, next to his nose, and slipped past his eyeball. It broke through his skull, but collapsed, telescoping inward and thankfully not damaging his brain. When he stood up and noticed what was stuck in his face, he tried to pull it out. His mother screamed as she watched it expand like an accordion, resembling Mary Poppins pulling a floor lamp from her purse.

On another occasion, a fifteen-year-old girl was admitted to the emergency room with a nail in her forehead after spending the day skating on her rollerblades. She had been carrying a wooden two-by-four with a nail in it when she suddenly tripped and fell. When she got up, the board was gone, but the nail was stuck in her forehead. She had to knock on a neighbor's door for help, but the neighbor passed out the moment she saw the nail, leaving the girl to call for an ambulance herself.

In a separate incident, a teenage boy took a routine trip out rabbit hunting with his .22 rifle on the rack of his Ford truck. He was standing on the curb when his friend grabbed the gun and accidentally pulled the trigger. The bullet traveled through the cab of the vehicle and entered the boy's head at his right temple, leaving an exit wound at his left temple. When the images from the CT scan came back, they didn't look good and showed metal debris, bone debris, and a large patch of damage. Lynn presented the boy's case to the other doctors during grand rounds and passed around the scans. Trauma and gunshot wounds were not unusual to the team, but Jason would be an exception.

"I want you to meet Jason," Lynn said. "Bring him in." The boy was pushed in on a wheelchair and placed in front of the main table. There, he stood up, walked around, and waved at everyone. Miraculously, he looked perfectly normal, despite the significant damage from the gunshot wound. "If the bullet had entered just an inch lower, he would have been toast," my dad told me.

I learned even the innocence of a pencil can cause serious trauma. One toddler had been drawing at a kitchen table when his mother saw him fall from the chair. She scooped him up and looked him over, noticing he looked fine, but when she picked the pencil off the floor, she saw it had broken in half and couldn't find the other piece. Examining him again, she found a scratch on his head, between his temple and right ear. She decided to have a doctor look at it and took him to Primary Children's, where a CT scan revealed the missing half of the pencil. He was admitted into surgery, where my dad cut open the area around the wound, but as he pulled the skin back, pressure from the boy's brain began pushing the pencil out of his head. Lynn quickly put his finger on the pencil to stop the progression, knowing it would be safe, and with a big smile on his face, said, "Quick! Someone take a picture!"

My dad was both a doctor and a father to my sister and me. He adhered to the moral code of not treating your own family, but if it was something he could easily take care of at home, he did. Anytime we accidentally slammed our finger in a car door and a blister would swell up under our fingernail, he would rummage through the medical supply basket in our laundry room and come out holding a fresh scalpel. These delicate knives are so sharp, that you can make a shallow cut without feeling a thing. Having a relatively painless knife is a blessing, but they filled me with fear for the same reason. Whenever I handled one, I constantly checked my arms and hands for gashes because I could slice myself open and not even know it. Thankfully, I never did, but that was most likely due to my extreme caution.

With all the antics of childhood, Alyssa took the trophy for giving our parents the most scares by repeatedly getting concussions. The earliest event was when we were about four years old, and she had just hopped out of the pool after a swim lesson. She slipped and hit her head on the concrete. "It sounded like a watermelon cracking open, and I've never been more scared in my life!" my dad said. "It sounded serious and knocked her out cold, so we scooped her up and piled into the car." My dad held Alyssa in the back seat as my mom drove us to the emergency room, but when she started waking up, they decided to change plans. "She's waking up, Mickey. I think she's going to be okay. Let's just take her home."

"Are you sure?" my mom asked.

"Yeah. We don't need a CT scan to tell us what we already know. If she's still out of it tomorrow, then we'll take her, but I think she'll be just fine." With that, we turned for home. Alyssa was very sleepy and started throwing up all over the backseat of the car, but my parents got her home, and she perked up a little while later. To this day, my dad looks back and considers that decision a serious breach of respectable parenting.

The second-worst time she hit her head was when my dad took us ice skating. We were eleven years old, and, like all beginning skaters, we fell regularly. On one fall, Alyssa came down harder than usual and hit her head on the ice, but a sign posted on the rink wall said, "If you fall, get up quickly." Usually, that would be sound advice since it's important to avoid being run over by other skaters; however, when you hit your head, the last thing you should do is "get up quickly." Alyssa heeded the sign by immediately standing up, which resulted in her passing out and hitting her head again, this time even harder. She definitely didn't get up quickly this time, not because she had learned her lesson, but because she was barely conscious. My dad helped her off the ice and draped her over an ottoman where we had laced up our skates. Selfishly, I wanted her to feel better quickly so I could keep skating, but she couldn't shake the nausea, and we had to take her home.

While we were pre-teens, we randomly passed out a few times, my sister more than me, which was possibly due to her history of concussions. Sometimes it could be explained, like when Alyssa locked her knees singing in church and fainted, taking out a few fold-out chairs with her. Other times not, like when I passed out brushing my teeth before bed, and my mother caught me before I hit my head on the tile floor. As long as you don't hit your head, waking up from being unconscious can be the most relaxing experience of your life. It sure was for me. It's an overwhelming feeling of peace in the darkness before the world comes back into view. However, if you hit your head, then you're waking up with a headache and possibly some nausea as a cherry on top.

I also passed out during a midterm exam in my eighth-grade English class, waking up draped over the desk behind me and my teacher's face staring down from above. The school's mistake was telling my dad I had experienced a seizure, and just like the kids in my class, they seemed to think those terms were interchangeable. Fainting can happen to anyone, and it doesn't mean anything is particularly wrong, but a seizure does not occur unless something *is* wrong. Not to mention, my dad's experience in the nervous system taught him that something could be seriously wrong, and it terrified him. Thankfully, it was not a seizure, but it didn't save me from the rumors my classmates spread. Funny enough, I thought the worst one was that the incident was caused by the stress of the exam. I was proud of my 4.0 GPA and didn't want anyone to think I wasn't prepared for that test.

A week after my sister got her ears pierced, around age ten, my mother was cleaning her fresh wounds with a cotton ball and attempting to dig out the earring post back that wedged itself inside one of the holes. Alyssa was already nervous, but my mother playfully tried to calm her down by showing her how little blood there was, which was just a drop on the tip of her finger. Needless to say, my sister's lights went out. She had been sitting on a barstool at our kitchen table when she slumped over onto my mom. "Lynn! Lynn, I need your help!" she shouted, knowing she couldn't hold Alyssa's dead weight for long. My dad flew down the stairs and helped carry her onto the couch, where we waited a few minutes for her to wake up. When she did, she was exceptionally frustrated that my mom hadn't finished removing the postback while she was still unconscious. Now they would have to start all over again.

My dad demonstrated his quick thinking when our family was vacationing in Mexico, and our family had stopped at a delicious-smelling restaurant. Alyssa had been wearing flip-flops like everyone else, but, as we followed the hostess up a small set of steps, she misplaced her foot and caught the nail of her big toe on the edge. Her nail was completely severed except for two prongs that extended from each side of the nail and went deep into the toe. We helped her over to a couch inside the restaurant, and I stared, fascinated, at the raw, bloody toe and how her nail was protruding at a ninety-degree angle. As she half-hyperventilated from the shock, my dad talked calmly to her and strategically kept her attention on their conversation before reaching down and ripping off the nail the rest of the way.

"AAHHHH!" she yelled.

"It had to come off anyway, Alyssa. Might as well do it while your body is in shock, so it's not as painful," he said. It wasn't until fifteen years later that he told me he had recently learned ripping off the nail had been unnecessary. "She could have kept the toenail," he said, "even though it was a lost cause and would only serve to protect the sensitive, raw skin while a new nail developed, she didn't need me to rip it off after all," he chuckled with a grin.

With all our mishaps, I'm surprised it took us until our senior year of high school to break a bone. Well, besides the broken nose Alyssa got falling from the playground equipment in kindergarten and having to hold a popsicle to it because the school was out of ice. When we were seventeen, she and I were attempting some Tae Kwon Do moves in a friend's yard late on a Friday night, and I stepped backward and tripped over the first step in a brick staircase. As I fell, I threw my left hand back to catch myself and felt an awful pain in my ring finger. My friends got me some ice, and then we continued with the rest of our evening.

My hand was still hurting when I got home, it was just after midnight, and my dad was fast asleep on the couch. I didn't want to wake him, but my hand was really talking, so I gently nudged his shoulder. He rolled over to see what was wrong.

"I hurt my hand," I said, holding it out to him. He seemed to give it an inspection, but in his drowsy state, I'm not sure if it was just for show, hoping I'd go to bed.

"Just take some ibuprofen," he said.

I did as he recommended and headed to bed. The next morning, I was still in pain, but my dad was at work at the local family practice clinic, so I performed my morning chores, watering and feeding the horses, goats, and chickens. Tossing hay was the most challenging since it required both my hands, but I got the chores done nonetheless. I showed up at my dad's clinic and perched myself in his office chair, waiting for him to round the corner once he had finished with his patient. When he walked in, I held up my left hand and said, "It still hurts."

"No problem," he said, smiling. "I'll get you an appointment with one of the other docs and we'll get it looked at." The fellow doctor examined my hand, squeezing it all over to see if I would jump, but I only winced a little.

"I'm sure it's not broken, but we'll get an x-ray just in case," he said.

I sat in my dad's office while I waited for the results of the x-ray when my dad and the other doctor walked in, holding the image and laughing.

"Well, it's broken!" they said, showing me the x-ray. I could see the damage to one of the bones inside my palm. "It's your fourth metacarpal, and it's not a simple break. What you've got is called a spiral fracture and as, you can see, the crack winds around the length of the bone like a corkscrew or winding staircase." They strapped me into a splint and sent me on my way.

One of my dad's kindnesses is making sure I get the best health care possible. Now with a broken hand, he took me to the office of an orthopedic surgeon, an elegant woman who wore stilettos under her lab coat. Before putting me in a cast, she asked me to do a quick test, having me close all my fingers into a fist. But instead of my fingers drawing down into my palm together, my ring finger curled under my pinky finger and poked out the side. Both my dad and I's eyes were wide in surprise, but the lady doctor was unphased.

"She's going to need surgery," the woman said. "Let's schedule her for tomorrow morning, first thing."

The next day, she installed six titanium screws, which seemed like a lot since the bone is only three inches long. After another week in a splint to let the swelling go down, she wrapped my hand in a florescent pink cast. She knew I wouldn't need the standard arm-length most kids got and, instead, gave me something resembling a fingerless mitten. I loved featuring it in my formal senior photos, even if I didn't have a cool story to go with it, like attempting to ride a rabid buffalo.

The second time I broke a bone, it was the same finger, but my dad's reaction was significantly different. There was a fresh blanket of snow on the ground, and we hitched up our sleds behind my mother's Clydesdales, attempting to drive the horses from the ground directly behind their thundering hooves. We bundled up in our winter gear and put jingle bells around the horses' necks for extra Christmas cheer. My mother and I took the driver's seats on the front sleds behind each Clydesdale and let my sister's kids pile onto the sleds behind us.

"Alright!" We rang in unison, with the word "alright" being the command for "walk." It's a word I habitually use in conversation, so I often feel the need to slap duct tape over my mouth when I'm with the horses to avoid accidentally giving them commands. When I'm sitting shotgun in my mother's wagon or show cart, I become an unintentional side seat driver.

As the horses picked up speed, their hooves started throwing chunks of compressed snow and mud at our faces, and, since we were in a horse pasture, I knew most of it must have included manure. Our horses and sleds flew across the field with a spray of snow streaming from either side, resembling the wake behind a Jet Ski. It was exhilarating to be at the reins of such powerful animals, which resembled wild mammoths in their shaggy winter coats, but we were also extremely vulnerable. A quick stop could send us straight into their legs or under their feet, which is never a place you'd want to be as they weigh 2,000 lbs. Nonetheless, we were right where we wanted to be with the wind in our faces and the beautiful views of the Wasatch mountains and a giant horse's butt. I could tell the horses were having as much fun as we were, but we couldn't sled for long. If the horses ran themselves into a sweat, then they'd freeze that night.

As we made our last few rounds across the pasture, the Clydesdale I was driving broke into a run, and I lost control. It headed for a wall of trees where I normally would have jumped ship, but I assumed my young nephew was still on the sled behind me. I clutched the reins in a grip of death, and I was yanked off my sled, being pulled through the snow and being forced to eat most of it. With one last, forceful jerk, the reins were ripped from my hands, and I slid to a stop. I watched my two sleds sail past me and was relieved to see my nephew had long since bailed.

My mother returned the Clydesdale, and the kids resumed sledding, but since my finger didn't seem quite right, I became the bench warmer. I could tell this break was in my actual finger, not the finger bone inside my palm like the first time. With the possibility of getting an x-ray, my dad laid out the options. "If it's broken, then we'll splint it. If it's not broken, then we'll splint it. We can get an x-ray, but either way, we're just going to splint it." As you can imagine, I skipped the x-ray and bought a splint.

I recently asked my dad what the scariest day of his life was, and he told me it was the day I had been sucked under a series of waves in Hawaii while we were on a family vacation. Alyssa and I had been eighteen, and our parents decided to take us to the tropics for Christmas. As much as I loved the sunny weather and green palm trees, Kevin McAllister was right; it didn't feel like Christmas without snow. Halfway through our trip, we found a beach bathed in a golden sunset, and there were only a moderate number of swimmers. Alyssa and I practiced our body surfing, but it wasn't long before I wanted to swim farther out and experience the bigger swells. I loved the ocean and felt confident in my swimming skills, having been on the school swim team. I saw a few other swimmers at the distance where I wanted to go, so I assumed it was safe. However, there is a significant difference between a city pool and the power of the ocean.

I headed out with my boogie board and was thrilled to be in the big swells, but soon I saw a wave approaching that was twice the height of the ones that came before. This wave looked formidable, and I knew I wouldn't have time to move before it crested over me. I remembered the counsel of swimming through a wave instead of swimming over it, so I grabbed my boogie board and pointed my arms in a streamlined pose. As it rolled into me, I tried to dive through to the other side, a move I had done countless times before, but never in a wave of this size or with a floatation device. The wave seized my board and pushed me up into the crest and down into a roll. I tumbled as the turbulence spun me like a washing machine. I thought the board's buoyancy would have brought me back to the surface, but it was held just as deep as I was. Letting it go was my next plan, but it was strapped to my wrist, and, through the confusion of the spinning, I was unable to untie it.

The gritty, sand-filled water scratched at my skin and seemed to fill my senses. I worried about hitting coral, which could inflict untold amounts of damage, and with each tumble, the cord to my board wrapped tighter around my wrist. After what felt like an eternity, I finally broke the surface and gasped for a lungful of air. For a moment, I was able to relax, thinking I could head back to the safety of the shore, but a moment later, I turned to see another huge wave come down on my head. I barely had enough time to grab a breath before it pulled me under once again. I turned end over end as the abrasive water sand-blasted my body, and I realized my boogie board was doing more harm than good. It was supposed to protect me and keep me afloat, but instead, it was spinning just as fast as I was, and unless I could unwrap the cord from my arm, it would hold me down there with it.

When I finally reached the surface for the second time, my heart sank as I turned and saw a third wave. I knew I couldn't swim to safety and worried I might not make it home. I couldn't free myself from this malicious pattern and didn't know how much longer I would last. However, as the third one took me down, I felt everything around me go quiet. My body continued to tumble, but the roar ceased and I felt alone with my thoughts. I realized this could be the end, and feared I might not see my family again. "Am I going to die?" I asked in prayer. A moment later, I felt a clear "No" answer back. It wasn't a sound but a feeling. "You will be okay. This isn't the end," it said. I felt a peace come over me, and it remained there until the wave rolled away. I surfaced for another desperate chest full of air, expecting to see another wave, but the horizon was flat, and the sea was still. I took my chance and swam back to shore, rushing across the sand into the arms of my parents. I cried into my beach towel as my dad rubbed my shoulders. He said, "As I was watching you out there, I couldn't tell if you were having the best time of your life or the worst."

Sitting in the sand, I watched the rhythms of the ocean and noticed the original waves had returned. After a while, the three huge waves came rolling in, followed by stillness. I now knew the pattern. Fifteen to twenty minutes of moderate-sized waves, three large ones, and then quiet. Repeat. Had I been attentive when I first entered the water, I would have avoided the large waves, and, even if they had caught me, I would have known there were only three. Nevertheless, I still consider my experience to be a miracle and am grateful I could leave the beach with my family that day.

18

The Plane from Hell

It was doomed from the beginning. Enough had gone wrong on that trip that saying my mother died a thousand deaths is conservative. "That piece of crap airplane," she said. Since Lynn's Piper Arrow had been purchased with two co-owners, he had to reserve it whenever he wanted to take it somewhere. Having put a California trip on the books, he was surprised to find the plane was missing when he opened the hangar. Sure enough, it was sitting at the main office hangar with its engine out. Lynn, Mickey, and two friends had already set their minds on going to California, so Lynn arranged for a rental. As they inspected the new plane, they noticed the upholstery was peeling off the ceiling, and one of the seats was leaning back and wouldn't come forward. As more red flags were popping up, Lynn called the owner. "Oh no, it's a great workhorse," the man said. "Not to worry. It's outstanding."

They decided to take the man's word for it, and soon the plane was off the ground. After refueling in Las Vegas,

Mickey looked out the window and saw the cars on the highway were moving faster than they were. It was a putsy plane for sure. Among the passengers was the flight nurse from Lynn's trip to "Dinosaurland," who kept her strawberry blonde hair hung neatly over her shoulder. That is until it got sucked out the window where the cabin seals were missing. She grabbed her hair and pulled it back in, clearly concerned about the state of the plane. Then the center of the map got sucked out.

The gauges weren't working either, including the fuel gauges on both tanks. The sky was already dark when they stopped in Santa Monica to drop off their other friend, but the small airport was closing.

"You won't have time to get your fuel and get out of here because the eleven o'clock curfew is upon us," an employee said. Lynn repeatedly ran the calculations to see if the remaining fuel would be enough to reach San Diego, with the protection of an hour's reserve, and each time the math said he had plenty. However, the gauges continued to read empty, and Lynn couldn't shake the gnawing doubt. Without enough time to refuel, the point seemed moot, so Lynn took to the murky skies once more.

By now, they were flying over open ocean, and the unreliable fuel gauge's "empty" sign was making everyone increasingly nervous. "Hang on," Lynn called over his shoulder, "I'm going to run one tank dry, so don't be disturbed if the engine cuts out." The moment the words left his mouth, the engine coughed, fizzled, and died. Nervously, he switched to the other tank.

"We're dead," Lynn thought to himself. Everyone except the flight nurse looked terrified. He saw an approaching airport, but the flashing beacons of white, white, and green warned them to stay away. It was a military base, and civilians were not allowed to land, even if they ran out of fuel. The only way this rental plane would be released was in pieces, boxed up on the back of a truck.

The group decided to risk a possible crash landing and head to the next airport on the outskirts of San Diego. They came in over the landing strip, and the plane started to sputter. They made it onto the blacktop and everyone gave a huge sigh of relief. Before they could get completely off the runway, the engine cut out, and they inched to a standstill.

"We're going to park right here," Lynn said matter-of-factly, giving the impression he had cut the engine on purpose.

"You're going to make us walk way over there to the hanger?" Mickey asked, bewildered. It wasn't a choice, but she didn't know that. Lynn was still playing it cool.

"There's no problem here!" he smiled.

Flying that rental plane wouldn't be the only risky call my dad would make as a pilot. On the way to a business meeting in Mesquite, Nevada, Lynn and Mickey were flying south over a beautiful valley between two of Utah's mountain ranges.

"I can't wait to reach the hotel," Mickey said. "The first thing I'm going to do is hit the pool."

"I'll have a couple of meetings to attend, but then I'll be right behind you. Save me a chair under an umbrella," Lynn replied.

"Thank you, again for flying us down. I enjoy these weekend trips," she said, but they weren't in the air long before the weather started to change.

"What are those clouds up ahead?" Mickey asked. "We've had spectacularly blue skies all day, and the news didn't say anything about bad weather."

"Those look like cumulus clouds," he said, staring at the mammoth-sized storm blocking his flight path. Its center was dark and looming but flush against the mountain.

"Should we go around it? It looks pretty daunting," Mickey stated.

"No, we'll be fine. It may look scary, but if we fly through, then we'll be out the other side in no time." He may have sounded practical, but in his thoughts, he looking at an adventure.

"Isn't there a saying that says, 'clouds have rocks in them'?" she asked.

"That's just an expression. It means cumulous clouds can be hard on planes, but most don't even have hail."

"All right, I'm trusting you."

As they entered the ominous, black monster, everything went dark, and visibility disappeared. It only took moments for Mickey to sense the danger and for Lynn to recognize he had made a mistake, but once again, he tried to play it cool.

"Don't worry about the lack of visibility," he said. "The gauges will tell us where we are and where we're going."

"But the gauges *aren't* working," she replied.

Suddenly, Lynn realized had forgotten to turn on the PITOT heat during the pre-flight check. Inside the nose of the airplane is a little air intake that feeds information to the gauges, but in cold, stormy weather, it needs a heater to keep the instruments from freezing over. On warm, sunny days, like what they had just left, the heater is unnecessary, but, since entering this icy monster, the instruments had frozen, and his gauges became useless.

To avoid alarming Mickey, he said, "Oh, here's the problem," and threw some unrelated switches. He knew full well how long the heater would take to thaw the instruments, and the plane would probably shoot out the other end of the storm before it did. That is if they made it that far.

"Don't worry. We should have readings any minute."

Lynn fought to keep the plane level, but it was no easy task with his sense of orientation left to the wind, and his stoicism was no longer subduing Mickey's sense of the danger. Spatial disorientation is a perilous vulnerability with one of the most common incidents being the death of Robert Kennedy. He too had been relying on his ability to see the landscape and, in his case, did not have the qualifications to fly strictly under his instruments. When the weather turned and dusk descended, basic landmarks were obscured and he lost his sense of direction. It's understandable to assume that a pilot can feel which direction he's going, especially if it's forward or straight down. However, when speaking with an experienced pilot, they can tell you that's not the case. Even a spiral dive, like the one Robert Kennedy experienced, is not always detectable. More than likely, he and his passengers didn't know they were plummeting toward the ocean until they hit it.

"Hang on! We'll be out soon!" Lynn called out.

As quickly as it had begun, the Piper Arrow pulled out from the darkness and into the bright rays of the sun.

"Don't you ever do that again!" Mickey said. "Now get us to Mesquite, so I can get out of this plane and put my feet back on the ground."

19

A Miracle

He shouldn't have survived. The level of brain injury dictated any attempts at saving this fifteen-year-old boy would be a fool's errand. He had been in the family's backyard arena, enjoying a ride on his favorite horse like he did every day after school when his father, Bob, got home. When Bob walked out to check on his son, he found him in the dirt, unconscious and convulsing in a seizure. The horse was standing quietly nearby, but, with no family or neighbors having seen the accident, Bob could only speculate what had happened. The boy's head was kinked at a strange angle, and Bob feared a broken neck. Brian was immediately taken to the local hospital where paramedics Life Flighted him to Primary Children's.

"I know you don't want to hear this," said an ER doctor, "but we don't believe he's going to make it through the night."

Bob froze where he stood. He stared at the doctor as if expecting him to change his answer. Bob's wife, brother, and the rest of his children were waiting inside a small room where families are kept after a traumatic accident. It was a mercy to be given privacy away from the bustle of the hospital. During the first few hours, the ER doctor periodically updated them. In his attempts to be sensitive, he was sugar-coating his words, but Bob was having none of it. He led the doctor outside the room to spare his family from the sobering question he desperately needed an answer to. When he returned, his family could see the heavy desperation on his face.

Upon admission, Brian was taken to the CT scanner for emergency images. Mickey was waiting for him and realized she knew his family when she saw the last name, Gowans. He was from our hometown, and his uncle, Gary, was our veterinarian; however, she didn't mention the connection and focused on Brian's care. A team of people helped Mickey prep Brian and laid him on the scanning bed. She knew an MRI would produce more detailed images, giving the doctors a better understanding of the damage, but the machine required at least thirty minutes to an hour, and she knew he didn't have that kind of time. If he were strapped inside the deep MRI tunnel, and he needed immediate help, no one would be able to reach him.

It was the start of an excruciatingly long night. As soon as the x-rays were done, the doctors swept him away and continued the fight to keep him alive. The wee hours of the morning approached, but Bob and Gary remained while the rest of the family had to return home. The lead neurosurgeon on the case was Dr. Moore who met with Bob to discuss the extent of the damage. He was a leader in his field, but Bob struggled to understand the medical jargon and felt lost from the moment they said, "Hello." Gary helped in the translation, pulling from his experience as a veterinarian, but it wasn't enough. Without a clear means of communication, Bob felt he was going to lose his mind.

Lynn had been on Brian's team from the minute the chopper landed on the rooftop but spent the first three days behind the scenes. As soon as there was a chance, he sat down with Bob and the family to make sure they understood what was going on. As was his custom, he spoke in layman's terms and made it easy for the family to get the answers they were looking for. After Bob had struggled to communicate with the other doctors, he saw Lynn as a Godsend.

"You need to know we've been giving him sedatives to keep him comatose," Lynn said. "When we feel it's safe for him to wake up, we'll ease him off, but we'd like to keep him on some of them. One of the reasons we're doing this, Bob, is because we don't want him to remember what he's going through. He'll still remember everything in his life up until he went unconscious during the accident, but we don't want him to remember any of this."

"Okay," Bob said. Then he thought to himself, "I wish I could have a shot of that myself."

Lynn and the team finally felt survival might be possible after three days of keeping Brian relatively stable. Although, only time would tell how much quality of life he would have. He was taken for his first set of thorough MRI images, and the doctors were able to see the full scope of the devastation. Lynn saw a massive volume of severed connections surrounding the boy's brain, a consequence of an abrupt deceleration, such as with a car crash. Brian was still in a coma, and they decided it was time to attempt a surgical miracle.

Most of the damage was deep in the center of his brain, while the pressure in his skull was mounting by the day. He was brought into the operating room where Lynn was tasked with relieving the pressure, but the question was how. Since all areas with spinal fluid are connected when the brain is under pressure, the spinal column is too. In any other case, relief is easily achieved by drilling a hole through the skull and inserting a drain into the cranial cavity. The worst plan would be to place a drain in the lower spine, like an epidural during childbirth, since there isn't enough room in the spinal column for the fluid to rush through. It would be like pulling the plug in a dam that's under tremendous pressure, which would herniate the brain and Brian wouldn't be able to recover from it.

It was a moment out of a medical drama where the patient is on the brink of death, and the doctor pulls a last-ditch Hail Mary in an attempt to save him. In theory, the idea shouldn't work, but, without any other options, the doctor attempts it anyway, and the patient survives. That was Brian Gowans. Lynn and the team were still unsure if he would live and were left with one extremely risky option to save him. Unfortunately, his brain was severely swollen, giving the team no fluid-filled ventricles to reach and making a drain in his skull impossible. The only choice left was to puncture the lumbar spine. It would be a mad man's idea, and everyone was thinking, "You're out of your mind." Lynn knew this boy would die if something drastic wasn't done, so he jumped on board and performed the puncture that could have hastened the boy's death but turned into the miracle they desperately needed.

The team now felt confident Brian would survive but still could not predict his quality of life or if his lifespan would be limited to years or months. Shortly after Brian's accident, the Gowans had ranching friends who experienced the same tragedy in their own family. Their twenty-one-year-old son had just returned from serving a two-year church mission and had been home for a mere two weeks when a similar incident occurred. The young man exhibited the same injuries, but, after he stopped responding to treatments, he was placed in long-term care and passed away just weeks later.

When Brian was pulled from his coma and the extent of the neurological damage was revealed, it was a disheartening reality. Speech was a battle, control of his arms was limited, and the doctors doubted he would ever walk again. His chances of survival had improved, but not enough to get him out of the woods. When he wasn't making enough progress after the surgeries and medication, it was suggested he be placed in a convalescence home like their friend.

"No, we're not moving him!" Bob repeated and vowed his son would return home where he belonged.

It was the beginning of a long 146 days in the hospital. Brian had spent four weeks in the ICU before being moved to a private room, and at least one family member remained at his side, taking rotations day and night. One night while watching Brian sleep, Bob wrapped himself tightly in a down winter coat. It was the middle of July, and the desert heat outside was oppressive, but, with Brian's body unable to control his temperature, the air conditioning in his room was cranked full blast, all while the nurses kept him draped in a wet sheet.

Mickey continued to take Brian's MRI scans each time the doctors needed an update and accompanied Lynn regularly when there was a moment they could break away and check on him. More than checking on Brian's progress, they just came to see him and make sure his family was holding up. Mickey brought a cheerful air to the room, an appreciated change from the stress and heartache that lingered there. Lynn continued to help them navigate the complexities of Brian's care and ensured there would be no stumbling over medical jargon, a formidable language of its own.

As Brian continued to recover, his physical therapy hit a roadblock. The long weeks in a hospital bed took a toll on his body, and his Achilles tendon had tightened, pulling his feet into ballet Pointe position and making him walk on his toes. A new surgery was performed, called a "heel drop," which lengthened the tendon, and Brian was able to resume his physical therapy once he healed. He was given a cast on each leg, and, for some curious reason, one was blue and one was pink.

Brian kept improving, and his parents were eventually allowed to take him on short day trips. The State Fairgrounds were bustling in the August heat, and the country music band, Rascal Flats, was in town. Bob and his wife, Tammy, took Brian to the concert, dressed in his favorite cowboy hat and shorts, which revealed his blue and pink leg casts. He still used a wheelchair but was happy to be somewhere familiar, smelling freshly bathed steers in the livestock barn and watching plates of funnel cakes walk by. By the time they returned to the hospital, it was late into the night, and the staff was up in arms. Bob and Tammy hadn't realized they were now in a partnership with the hospital as Brian's caretakers and chuckled at how bent out of shape they were over their middle-of-the-night return.

"When Brian goes home and you start life again, he's going to struggle," Lynn said the following day. "He'll be able to remember everything up to the accident. Everything he ever did, every game, being on the swim team, and riding each day after school. More impactfully, he'll remember what it was like to be independent."

Bob sighed. "That's okay. It's better than the original prognosis, so we'll take it."

"Keep up the physical therapy, and he should be able to ride again."

"But we were told there was too much brain damage, and we couldn't risk further injury," Bob said.

"That's true unless he wears a helmet."

"I don't think that'll ever happen."

"I know of a cowboy hat that has a helmet built into it. I'll get him one."

Brian was finally able to leave the hospital and return home. He continued to improve and started riding again, wearing the new helmet he calls his "Hoss Hat," a name given for its resemblance to a character's hat on the television show *Bonanza*. He earned school credit for his extensive physical therapy and graduated on time with the rest of his high school class. With the help of his dad, Brian walked across the stage and received his diploma.

20

International Cases

Calls came in from around the world, including the Vatican, Egypt, and Honduras. At the time, pediatrics was still a cutting-edge field, and many countries couldn't afford the luxury. Even more rare was the specialty of pediatric neurosurgery, a field that was still in its early stages of advancement. Whenever an international conference was held, the community of worldwide pediatric neurosurgeons was small enough that everyone knew everyone else. It made it easy for a hospital to find help because their department would already know the major players around the world.

A rabbi in New York was looking for help on behalf of a child in Israel. He was a concierge-of-sorts and part of an international network for "Where do I take my kid?" Knowing the child needed surgery, the rabbi scoured the latest medical journals in search of the most recent paper on this particular kind of tumor removal. What he found was an article by Dr. Jack Walker and immediately called Primary Children's.

"Put this boy on Dr. Walker's schedule for Friday morning," he said.

"Yes, sir," his assistant replied.

Twenty minutes later, the rabbi called back.

"Did you do it?"

"Yes, sir."

Lynn was especially excited for this child's arrival because he thought his ties with the local Jewish Community Center would help connect the patient to the people and resources she needed. However, the rabbi wanted nothing to do with the Jewish communities in America, and the child was cared for by the people who traveled with her. Due to the strict kosher diet and other requirements, Lynn realized neither he nor the hospital could assist her with food or anything else.

Years later, while Lynn was on call late one night, he got paged by the operator who said, "Lynn, the Vatican is on the phone and wants to talk to you."

"Me?? Okay, put them on."

He spoke with a representative from the Vatican who described a young adolescent with a brain tumor in the back of the head. Much like the rabbi, the man said, "The last person to publish something on this kind of tumor was Jack Walker. We want to send the child to you."

"Alright," Lynn said. "Would you mind reading the MRI report to me?"

Lynn listened to the report, and then said, "Hey guys, I know you want to bring him here, and we'd love to have you, but Dr. Di Rocco is located in Rome, and he can easily take care of this." Lynn had met Dr. Rocco on several occasions while traveling for medical conferences and knew a flight from Europe to Primary Children's was unnecessary. The Vatican called the referred doctor, and the procedure was successfully performed locally, saving the child a lengthy trip across the ocean.

A few months ago, while I sat with my dad in his living room, he caught me admiring the vibrantly painted Russian nesting doll perched on the log mantle above the fireplace. It had been there for as long as I could remember, but I hadn't realized there might be a story behind it.

"Do you know where that came from?" he asked.

"No," I said.

"It was a gift by a physician from Moscow who brought her child to be treated in the US. The boy had been born with spina bifida, a commonly treated birth defect where a baby's spine didn't close completely during development, causing a variety of problems like poor mobility, lack of bladder function, and leaking spinal fluid from his back. If it's left untreated, these babies eventually die from a brain infection, usually while they're still very young.

"In countries like Russia, governments often won't spend money on a 'wasted cause,' and, in this child's case, they refused to let him be treated. The mother flew him to Utah where I got to help with the case. He was eight years old and well past the normal life expectancy of an untreated patient, but our team jumped in, and the procedure was performed with ease."

Early in his career, my dad began accompanying Jack Walker to international medical conferences, learning the latest developments, and networking with foreign doctors to better help the patients. He quickly realized that flying business class was a vacation in and of itself. On a trip to Austria, they rode a 747, one of the jumbo jets with a second level. There were no cubicles, just big chairs and open spaces. As Lynn sat in his window seat, he stretched his arm out to see if he could touch the glass from where he sat. He couldn't. The flight attendants pulled his shoes off and replaced them with soft, heated socks, and carved slices of prime rib while laying them gently on his plate. He ate with fancy, metal silverware and drank several glasses of champagne. They would be in Austria for only three days, which wasn't long enough to shake the jet lag, but Lynn and Jack relished being away from the office. This was all while the rest of the department was working hard in their absence and half-wishing the two of them were dead.

The first medical conference Lynn attended took him to Istanbul. Eager to go, he had studied all he could about Mesopotamia, the Turkish armies, and the sultan. On the outbound flight, he excitedly told Jack he would be keeping a journal. "Really?" Jack asked. He didn't want to be a part of anyone's journal. Once they arrived in-country, Jack stepped out of a steam-filled bathhouse, momentarily leaving Lynn to lounge in the luxurious pool alone. As in any traditional Turkish bath, they had been stripped of their clothes and each wrapped in a thin cotton towel. Then, they were treated to a series of progressively warmer pools while being guided by bathing attendants who scrubbed them down with handwoven wash clothes. After a foam wash and a massage, they chose to linger in the bath for some relaxation.

"This is just like a harem, but without the harem!" Lynn thought.

A moment later, as Lynn soaked up the peaceful tranquility, a woman walked in and strolled up to the pool's edge where he was sitting. Without saying a word, she dropped her bathrobe at her feet, revealing every inch of her body, and then turned and walked along the pool before slipping out the door in the back.

"Jack! Get back here!"

Their accommodation, the Ciragan Palace, was an impressive sight. Formerly an Ottoman palace built for the sultan, its tall archways framed stone walls where ornate paintings and Persian rugs hung. Luxurious rooms filled with red and gold furniture overlooked a cabana-lined swimming pool, and residents could sip their black tea while gazing across the Bosphorus, a natural waterway dividing Europe from Asia. It had the old world feel Turkey is famous for.

The medical conference was held near the country's southern border, but, when their business was complete, they ventured north to Istanbul. Jack was game for any cultural experience the locals handed him and made sure camel riding was no exception. The latest of these cultural ventures was the Turkish bathhouse where Lynn was sitting in the warm pool and staring at the robe in front of him. As soon as Jack appeared, Lynn whispered as loud as he could, "Get your butt in here. You've gotta see who belongs to this bath towel!" They sunk back into the water and waited. Their skin shriveled into prunes, but she never returned.

On every trip they took, they smoked Cuban Cohiba cigars. "Best on the planet," my dad told me while closing his eyes and smiling. He inhaled deeply, as if the thought took him back to those moments, relishing the perfect balance of smooth and flavorful Cuban tobacco. I glanced at the yellow "Cohiba Cigar" t-shirt he was wearing and chuckled at how timely the moment was. He often smoked one in the yard when he had friends over, but one day our Great Dane, the Duke of Earl, thought they were hot dogs. Well, they definitely were hot. Jack and my dad were standing next to each other when Jack lowered his cigar to his side and Duke lunged at the opportunity. Our poor pooch gave himself a good burn in his mouth and never did that again.

While on the Turkey trip, Jack and Lynn wanted to mess with the department team back home, so they taped their Cohiba wrappers to a letter and faxed it to them. They addressed it specifically to Joe Petronio, whom they had left in charge of covering their duties. It simply read "Jack's" and "Lynn's" with arrows pointing to their respective cigar labels. "Thinking of you!" was scribbled at the bottom.

Dr. Jack Walker with Hal Rekate

Whenever there was a local conference in the Intermountain region, Jack hired Lynn to pilot the team to places like Boise, Pocatello, and St. George. Lynn wasn't there as a medical professional, just a private pilot who got to hang out with the nurses while the team visited different clinics. Instead of taking his own plane, he rented a Cessna 310, because it sported twin engines and could carry two extra people. One day, he explained to me the rule of thumb regarding the number of engines versus the elevation. "If a plane with two engines loses one, the remaining engine can only keep the plane 3,000 feet above sea level. The Salt Lake Airport is 4,200 feet above sea level, so the local joke goes, 'What's the difference between a single-engine plane losing an engine and a twin-engine plane losing an engine? The twin engine is a noisy descent while the single is quiet. Either way, both planes are comin' down.' Thankfully, the Cessna 310 had enough power to keep us airborne with or without a failed engine."

21

Tragedy

At Primary, one of the first cases Lynn was given was a young boy named Scott Murdock who was recovering from brain cancer that had recently been removed. He was raised in Pinedale, Wyoming, the hometown of fellow ski patrolman Stuart Thompson, and was the son of a cowboy who embodied old-school cattle ranching. If there was an Olympic medal for the manliest, grizzled mustache, his father would have been undefeated. In contrast, his mother was a petite, red-haired English teacher from Scotland who was just as hard-working and tough in the frigid Wyoming climate as her husband. The family regularly drove the four hours to Primary Children's for Scott's post-surgery check-ups and quickly befriended Lynn, a connection sparked by their mutual friend, Stuart. Mickey had been performing Scott's MRI scans from the beginning and grew close to the family as well.

During these trips, the Murdock family would often stay in our home, and Scott became like a big brother to Alyssa and me. When he was in the fifth grade, he and his mother came to visit after Scott had returned from a Florida beach with his cousin. His back resembled a freshly boiled lobster, and his mother smeared Desitin all over and carefully laid a t-shirt over top. The cream smelled of cod liver oil, and Scott was so exhausted he nearly fell asleep at the dinner table.

"Why don't you go to bed?" his mother, Madeleine, asked.

"You're welcome to help yourself to the guest bedroom upstairs," my mother offered. "It'll be on your left."

Scott slogged his way upstairs and crawled into the first bed he found and fell asleep. He was completely unaware he had collapsed into my parent's bed, reeking of fish oil. "You mother was mortified," he later recounted, but my dad reassured her. "Don't worry about it at all. We'll sleep on the couch."

Decades later, people continue to offer Scott their condolences when they hear of his childhood bout with cancer. "No, it was a good experience," he said. "The friendships I gained were an excellent trade, and I'd pay it again. Besides, I think it's harder to be on the sidelines than to be the patient." To this day, Scott and his family believe he would not have survived his cancer had he been born ten years earlier. "Jack Walker and the rest of the neurosurgical team were forging ahead in work that had never been done before," Scott said. "They were the medical equivalent of AC/DC!"

Out on the slopes of Alta one day, our families were skiing together and heading down a flat, snowcat track. While gliding down the hill, my dad lifted his right ski, twisted it around, and set it down opposite his left foot with his legs crossed. For the moment, his legs looked like a pretzel. While still sailing down the slope, he then lifted his left leg, twisted it, and set it back down next to his right leg, bringing him into a backward-facing position. During the entire maneuver and now skiing backward, he was giggling like a little kid, and everyone else couldn't help but laugh along with him.

"He is the most unlikely character," Scott would tell me years later. "He's more of an overgrown kid than the serious academic usually seen in an operating room. How is this guy even allowed in a hospital if he's not being admitted?" He laughed, "Let alone be on one of the premier neurosurgical teams in the world?" As I grew up, I began to understand the deep level of respect our families have for each other because whenever the Murdocks are brought up in conversation, my parents use a kind of reverence that I have yet to hear when they speak of anyone else.

Years later, Scott's father, Stan, was in a horse-riding accident while attending to his cows early one morning. He was found paralyzed, face-down in a puddle, but a ranch hand was able to roll him over just before he drowned. A medical helicopter took him to the remote town of Idaho Falls to seek emergency treatment while many Pinedale residents berated Madeleine for not having him taken to Salt Lake City. Lynn immediately traveled to Idaho to inspect the hospital and speak with the spinal surgeon. He reassured both Madeleine and Scott that they had made the right choice.

"The ICU here is far superior to the overcrowded conditions in Salt Lake, and the surgeon is a leader in his field," he said. Scott noticed Lynn and the surgeon's bald heads, which revealed extensive scarring from their own serious injuries. He watched the two men standing head-to-head, discussing his father's condition, and drew Madeleine's attention to their scars.

"If experience has anything to do with it, I think these two are the most qualified to decide on Dad's treatment." It was a valiant fight, but despite everyone's best efforts, Stan never made it home. Like the tough cowboy he was, he held on for an entire year before passing away.

While my sister and I were little, our dad would tiptoe into our bedroom to say goodnight, no matter how late it was. Like most nights, it was well past our bedtime and I was half asleep. I watched Alyssa doze, a motionless lump under her covers, as the moon cast its rays across the floor. I heard the door creak open, and my dad appeared, but, as he walked in, I could tell something about this night was different. He quietly knelt at my bedside and laid his head in his arms on my quilt. No words were spoken, and I wondered what could be wrong as I lay there in the stillness. Eventually, he lifted his face and looked at me with a weary expression.

"Two of the patients I'd been taking care of were twins and about your age."

I smiled.

"We lost them today. We did everything we could, but it wasn't enough."

I had never seen my dad so heartbroken. He had lost patients before, but this one hit too close to home. He quietly wrapped me in his arms and gave me an extra tight hug before kissing me goodnight. While writing this book, I asked him about the patients he had lost. "It's hard to remember things you've spent a lifetime trying to forget," he replied. "But there were so many."

TV dramas often place a theatrical light on grieving families who have just received devastating news, such as collapsing into each other's arms, crying, or wailing. But in real life, it's quite the opposite. Whenever my dad had to inform a family that their child had a grim diagnosis or had passed away, the news was met with stunned silence. Once thoughts could be gathered, usually denial followed. One of my dad's hardest experiences was when my cousins rushed into the hospital to see how their brother was doing after being Life Flighted in. He had been struggling with a bad case of the flu, and no one expected the need for hospital admission, let alone an emergency helicopter. It was nearly impossible to explain that their brother hadn't made it to the hospital in time. He had died in the air.

Whether my dad was in his early years and pushing the limits up a near-vertical cliff, or in the middle of his medical career and removing a malignant tumor from a young child's head, he was drawn to the limit of the human condition. Whether his own or that of someone else's, he had the tendency of keeping life in his hands. In the past, he put life on the line for an exciting thrill but now fought each day to preserve it. The invincibility of youth had faded, and he had seen more suffering and death than most see in a lifetime. His priorities had shifted into caring for his patients and family, and never in his life did he have this much to lose.

22

Conjoined Twins

UFO-shaped lights hovered overhead, sending wide beams onto the operating table. A crowd of doctors and nurses surrounded two babies who had waited patiently for this groundbreaking surgery. Conjoined twins, Amanda and Andrea, had been flown in from Chile with their mother, seeking a highly specialized surgery. Siamese twins are rare, but babies joined at the head are even more so, occurring approximately once in 1,250,000 births. That's only two percent of an already rare condition. The majority of conjoined twins are attached at the abdomen and are separated by an entirely different kind of surgical team, but Amanda and Andrea were attached at the head, bringing the case to Primary Children's department of neurosurgery.

As the resident PA, Lynn was the gatekeeper to the brain, opening up heads for Jack or another neurosurgeon to dive in, but this case was a mammoth-sized task and mostly unprecedented. Lynn contributed as part of the think tank, helping design and plan each surgery, but left the hands-on work to the most experienced on the team. Standing around these two babies, the whole team looked on as one of the doctors delicately began the surgery. Lynn knew this would be the first of many surgeries, and there would be no room for error.

An anatomical model was built so the team could see everything in 3D while they mapped out plans for each surgery. The challenges were immense, and, if they tried to separate the twins too quickly, the girls could go into shock and die. Instead, the surgeons would work a little bit here and a little bit there, letting the babies heal for a few weeks before heading back to the operating room. However, the surgeries were often long and exhausting, an arduous effort for everyone involved.

"It was a welcome break in the monotony," Lynn said. "Even though trauma is never monotony, it's still routine. Not many neurosurgeons can say they've separated Siamese twins." Congenital defects, like Spina bifida, have varying degrees of severity, but the procedures to fix them are essentially the same. The project to separate conjoined twins is a whole new kettle of fish and like nothing Lynn had ever seen before. The babies didn't share any brain tissue, which was a tremendous blessing, but new skull bone would have to be grafted from their ribs to cover where the connection had been. It took over a dozen surgeries, six of which were strictly to separate blood vessels, and the press was watching every step of the way. "It has been a marathon, but we're ready to press on," Jack reported to a local newspaper. Headlines ran from coast to coast as families throughout the nation followed the girls' progress.

The final separation took place on the twins' first birthday. When the surgery was well underway and the only connection between the babies was a small network of blood vessels, the team encountered a major problem. While Amanda was doing well, Andrea took a turn for the worse. Everything the intensive care unit did to help the struggling baby resulted in the opposite effect. When Amanda's blood pressure went up, Andrea's would drop, and when Amanda's blood pressure would drop, Andrea's went up. Each baby took turns flat-lining and requiring resuscitation.

As the team fought to keep them alive and pull them through the last stretch of surgery, a nurse finally piped in, "You know, every time you try to boost one of the baby's vitals, it has the reverse effect. Why don't you try the opposite? Instead of giving the failing baby the boost, give it to the healthy one." The intensive care unit doctor replied, "That is the stupidest thing I've ever heard. Let's try it." It worked. The babies completed their marathon of surgeries and took some well-earned rest while under the watchful care of Jack's team. In time, they flew home with their mother and were reunited with their family.

The longest surgery Lynn ever participated in lasted forty-eight hours. Jack had a cot in the back room where he managed to grab a few hours of sleep, but the anesthesiologists had teams, allowing them to take turns. The patient was a Polynesian girl from Arizona who had bleeding in her head. It was normal to see patients with veins and arteries that weren't fully developed or vascular tumors that bled a lot, but this girl had both.

She was on the operating table for what felt like an eternity. Every time Lynn and the rest of the surgical team thought they were done, they would push her bed down to radiology and take images to double-check, not an easy feat when you're leaving essential equipment in the OR. Pulling a patient out of an operating room has been likened to undergoing a moonwalk. "Nope. Still a little bit left," they would say, and have to cart her back up to continue the marathon.

By the time the work was complete and it was Lynn's turn to close her up, the girl's scalp was two inches thick with black necrosis. The team hadn't expected such a lengthy procedure and hadn't attended to the skin folded over her face as they otherwise would have. The necrosis was repairable, but it was a gruesome job. Lynn scraped and scraped the dead flesh until fresh blood streamed from healthy tissue. The swelling made stitching her scalp back together a significant challenge, but Lynn patched her back up, and she made a full recovery.

As Lynn made his rounds through the hospital, visiting neurosurgery patients in their rooms, he knocked on the door of a six-month-old girl and walked in to greet her young mother. The infant had just been admitted with severe symptoms of hydrocephalus, which left her skull swollen like a balloon and her forehead bulging from the pressure inside. It gave her an appearance more like a space alien than a normal infant, and the pressure was causing her eyes to point down, a term called "sunsetting."

"We have her scheduled for surgery tomorrow morning, and we'll take good care of her," Lynn said. "A drain will be placed in her head, and soon her skull and eyes will begin to return to normal."

"Any idea what caused it?" she asked.

"It's usually a tumor but can be hereditary. In your daughter's case, she was simply born with the condition, but don't worry, it's something we see every day, and she should go on to live a normal life. Unfortunately, these drains, called shunts, sometimes fail after a while, so let us know if she starts experiencing headaches again."

In Lynn's experience, not all parents embraced the treatments suggested by the hospital or western medicine in general. On occasion, homeopathic families would treat their children alongside the doctors, hanging charms on their beds and giving them herbs. One child was mysteriously not eating until a dietician realized his parents had been stuffing him so full of herbs that he couldn't stomach anything else.

A patient named Daniel became known as one of the Four Horsemen of the Apocalypse. He had a drain in his head, and his mother regularly brought him in for relief from his terrible headaches, which were a sign the drain wasn't working. The team took CT scans, but the images showed no unusual buildup of spinal fluid, signaling a fully functional shunt. Since there is no way to prove a patient is in pain, the team had to trust his headaches were genuine. The boy underwent many surgeries over the years to relieve the pain.

At times, the mother called late at night on her son's behalf. "He's in terrible pain. Should I pick him up a prescription or bring him to the ER?"

"No, don't come to the ER. We'll fax the prescription."

It wasn't until the department assigned their neurosurgical nurse, Kathy, to investigate his chart that the red flags became apparent, and the total number of surgeries was calculated. It was 126. His mother repeatedly asked for her son to be provided with narcotics, but it's likely those pills never made it to the boy.

It was believed the mother had been taking them herself, and she was using her son to feed the addiction. It was also Primary's policy to require at least one CT scan before any operation, amounting to an equal number of scans for Daniel. All for his mother.

Later in Lynn's career, there would be many patients who would come looking for narcotics. It was an epidemic in every clinic and hospital across the country, but Lynn learned to mitigate the problem by adhering to the policy of "Don't feed the birds." Addicts are skilled at sniffing out doctors who liberally prescribe pain meds, but once Lynn built a reputation, the flow slowed significantly. When he told a patient no, they sometimes turned mean or furious, but he took good care of those with genuine pain problems and only prescribed what was necessary. As for the other cases, he became proficient at sifting out the B.S.

23

Cats that Need Fixin'

"Mayday! Mayday!" a woman cried over the marine radio, giving her location on the lake and asking for the Bullfrog Park Rangers. With only silence following each of her pleas, Lynn, Mickey, and their group knew they had to step in. Scott Droubay, a friend and the owner of the ski boat they were using, picked up the radio and asked if they could help.

"Yes! My husband is badly hurt!"

"Where are you?" he asked. The woman relayed her location and Scott realized they were only

a short distance away.

"We're on our way!" he said, revving the engine and speeding through the canyon to find her. Lake Powell is an intricate reservoir built in the middle of Southern Utah's desert and lined by tall, red rock plateaus and sheer-faced cliffs. Viewed from the sky, it looked more like a bad case of spider veins than a lake, and it would be easy to get lost in its countless canyons, especially when the surface of the water creates a kaleidoscope effect.

As they turned a corner, they found a fancy ski boat and a woman waving her arms. She quickly ushered Lynn and Mickey on board where they found her husband sitting, half-conscious, and yelling at his three young daughters who were huddled and crying in the bow below deck. Nothing he said was making any sense, and they recognized right away he was delirious.

"Can you tell me what happened?" Lynn asked the woman, kneeling and giving her husband a thorough look.

"We were pulling him on an inner tube behind our Wave Runner, but when we turned to avoid hitting a canyon wall, the rope snapped and sent him straight into the rock face," she said, and Lynn turned to see tears streaming down her cheeks.

Back on the other boat, Scott was able to get ahold of the authorities and radioed in for help. With a helicopter on the way, Lynn continued to examine the man and noticed his forehead had been pushed in, and spinal fluid was leaking from his nose. The bones in his hand also appeared to be broken where he had attempted to shield his face during the crash. Fearing a broken neck and to prevent further injury, Lynn and Mickey laid the man down with Mickey using her arms to brace his head and neck. For forty-five minutes, she held him, even as he groaned with nausea. Their calming presence helped settle the near panic that had risen on the ski boat.

As a helicopter came swooping in overhead, the propellers sent gusts of wind over the top of them and roughed up the water's surface. Without a solid place to set it down, the pilot balanced one skid on a rock nearby. Two medical professionals hopped off the chopper and helped Lynn and Mickey carry the man from the boat to a rock and then to the helicopter. As they strapped him in, Lynn noticed one of the medics was a PA like himself. Suddenly, the patient threw up all over the inside of the bird, and Lynn was grateful his job was done.

During the flight and over the next several days in the hospital, the man's condition was touch and go. There was swelling in his brain, temporary blindness, and an immense number of cuts and gashes. He stopped breathing several times, so they hooked him to a ventilator. Nevertheless, he persevered. Lynn and Mickey visited him at the hospital and were encouraged to see his progress. Despite the doctor's prediction of a long stay, he improved enough to return home two weeks later. It was a slow recovery, but a few months later, the couple visited Lynn at his office to thank him for coming to their aid. The husband's speech was slow and deliberate, but they expressed waves of gratitude for his safety and continued improvement.

Although Lynn's place of work was Primary Children's, his employer was the University of Utah, which found itself undergoing significant budget cuts and mass layoffs. Since the position of a PA in the neurosurgical department was not deemed an absolute necessity, Lynn was transferred to a new position at a family practice clinic outside a rural farming community. He had now returned full circle to the life he had planned in PA school. Lynn now worked a job that had closing hours and time off for holidays. The clinic was a mere ten-minute drive from our home and a considerable improvement from the forty-five-minute commute around a mountain range and through the city. It was also the first time I can remember having both my parents home for Christmas since in previous years they had taken turns sharing the demanding schedule alongside the rest of Primary's staff.

At the clinic, every appointment was a puzzle to be solved, and my dad enjoyed the challenge. It wasn't as satisfying as working at Primary, saving children's lives alongside a team of his best friends, but it meant he could spend more time with his family. There were no more days or nights on-call and no more twenty-four-hour shifts. He enjoyed caring for the residents of his community, and, even if he didn't know a patient directly, it was fun to find the tie through family or friends that connected them. When Mickey also transferred from Primary Children's to our small, local hospital, she too enjoyed caring for the locals. Like my dad, her transition was more than geographical, and she moved from caring strictly for children into the field of mammography.

My dad became the most efficient doctor at the clinic, keeping wait times and his stack of unprocessed paperwork to the bare bones. But he also had a calm and gentle bedside manner that made each patient feel like his priority. When he entered an exam room, he sat down and gave his full attention with no pressure to rush. He loved the kids and older youth, although telling teenage girls that they're pregnant was not his favorite thing. Whenever he had a teenager with the perception of invincibility, he liked to offer a reality check. "If you don't wear a seatbelt while driving, the chances of you dying are low, it's true. However, chances are high you'll end up in a wheelchair for the rest of your life while someone changes your diaper and wipes your butt every day." Those messages seemed to be heard loud and clear.

As he learned to care for patients of every age, it brought an unexpected challenge for him. When working at a children's hospital, death is never an option, and no effort is spared. However, at the family clinic, Lynn had to adjust to the finality that life eventually reaches its end and death is not always the enemy. The elderly brought other challenges too, like when they came in complaining of abdominal pain, which was hard to test for and could be caused by a thousand different scenarios.

Lynn discovered that doctors at family clinics usually work as lone wolves, operating independently and having their own patients. Although they were happy to help when one of them needed assistance, like the day a young boy came in needing stitches on his forehead while Lynn had been struggling with low blood sugar that afternoon. He called in Dr. Gavin Van Staden, a fellow clinic doc and transplant from South Africa who specialized in recovery dives when emergency teams were looking for a body.

"Gavin, can you sew this kid up? I can't hold a needle straight today."

"Oh, I'd be pleased to do so."

Sales reps for drug companies appeared frequently, filling the conference room with tacos, pulled pork sandwiches, and the like. Lynn patiently listened during the meetings, hearing the benefits of their medication, but the salesmen might as well have saved themselves the tacos because, in the end, Lynn only prescribed what he thought was best for his patients. Decades ago, those same companies went as far as giving out tickets to Broadway, but eventually, the tactic was shut down since it appeared too much like bribery.

While free samples were still being given away in droves by the pharmaceutical companies, doctors could supply medications to their patients for years without buying a single pill. While Lynn was fresh out of training, he worked under a physician at a family clinic that had an office filled with shelves of medications provided entirely free. The doctor was collecting as much as he could and giving it to his patients whose families could not afford it.

Lynn loved being a PA, but not in an emergency room. Nearing retirement, he split his time between two locations; one was reasonably pleasant, but the other was not. One afternoon, a ten-year-old girl came in with an abrasion on her knee, and Lynn watched as an imposing nurse attended to her. Like Lynn, the nurse was a former Navy Corpsman, but he had a terrible bedside manner. As Lynn glanced over at the injury, he knew the girl would need a tetanus shot, but the hulking nurse marched over and waved an enormous needle in her face. She screamed and began backing over one exam bed after another. "Would you rather die?!" bellowed the nurse. All the while, the girl's mother showed no signs of calming the situation. She wasn't cheering for the nurse but was completely compliant with his behavior. Lynn made sure the nurse was fired shortly after.

As the neighborhood doc in a rural area, my dad regularly had friends and farmers calling on him, asking for advice and the occasional house call, which he happily gave for free. He kept our laundry room stocked with surgical towels, hemostats, scalpels, and other leftovers from Primary Children's operating rooms. Whenever a tool or towel is set out for surgery, it's considered no longer sterile even if it was never used. My dad prevented these materials from going to waste by bringing them home, saving some for us, and giving the majority to Gary Gowans for his vet clinic. There was no expectation of quid pro quo, but when we realized our barn cat population was out of control, my dad had to make a call.

Our family was the beneficiary of many abandoned pets, and I'm sure most people saw our farm animals and thought, "They probably won't notice one more." Usually in the form of a kitten, they would appear on our front porch, meowing for shelter and a meal, which my sister and I happily provided. As a child, I adored when these tiny furballs showed up and realized the tales of storks bringing babies must have been misinterpreted. Storks bring kittens.

We kept only one cat indoors while the rest lived in the barn, well-fed by Meow Mix as they hunted gophers and mice for sport. On two occasions, I found dead snakes in the yard with hundreds of tiny puncture wounds and determined their cause of death must have been a cat. The trouble began a couple of years after the strays started showing up, and we realized they were breeding. By the time my dad estimated we had thirty cats, he and my mom knew drastic measures needed to be taken to curb the growing population. My dad figured if he could perform surgery on a human, then spaying and neutering a few cats should be easy. "So what if I lose a few with the learning curve," he joked. "They're just cats." He got online and began researching the surgeries, but it was still the late 1990s, and the internet wasn't very helpful yet. He used keywords like "Instructions to fix cats," but the results turned up a picture of a shotgun.

"Hey Gary, would you teach me how to spay and neuter cats? I've got a bushel full over here, and they need fixin'."

"Sure, I'd be happy to," he said, but after a few days called back. "You know what, just let me do it."

"All right, when would you like them?"

"Friday."

"How many would you like at a time?"

"What?" Dr. Gowans probably regretted making that free deal once he realized how many we had. We brought five every Friday, five weeks in a row. He asked us to keep them in groups of the same gender, but we didn't always get it right. It's hard to tell sometimes.

One of our neighbors, Debbie Bodell, would call in the middle of the night looking for medical advice, but one night she had an unusual request.

"My husband, Scott, has been kicked in the head by a horse. Can you come over and take care of him?"

"Call 911!" my dad said.

"Oh no, he's okay. It's not that big of an emergency."

My dad walked across the quiet, country street to their home where he found the man sitting in his living room with an ugly, dirty gash on his forehead.

"It looks nasty but it isn't deep," my dad said. "I feel confident you're going to be just fine."

"Is there anything you can do?" Scott asked.

"It needs to be stitched up; there's no question about that. I have a surgical stapler at home and am happy to take care of it, but the problem is, I don't have any anesthetic. Not to mention, staples are never supposed to be put in someone's face because they scar like crazy. Your choices are either me or the ER."

"Let's do it."

"Just don't tell anyone who put staples in your face."

Scott was ready for him when my dad returned with the white, disposable surgical stapler.

"Cachink."

"Ahhh!"

"Cachink."

"Ahhh!"

My dad put six staples across the wound. When he was finishing up, he noticed a few cowboy tears trickling down the man's cheeks.

"You'll need to have these removed in three days."

Five days later, Scott called to say he was ready. That's when my dad walked into our living room where I was lying on the floor in my fleece, zip-up-the-front pajama dress, and watching Animal Planet before bed. I was still in eighth grade when he handed me a pillow and punched six surgical staples into it. He then handed me the tool to remove them, which looked like the nail clippers we used on our dogs.

"Try taking these out."

He had a grin on his face, so I knew he was up to something, and I was excited to be a part of it. I had no idea what this was about, but I gave it my best shot. When we were younger, he let us punch these staples into gaping tears in his old Toyota Corolla, whom he called the Poodledink, after the little sausages served at the Buckhorn mess hall at Alta. The car's upholstery had huge holes, and Alyssa and I attempted to patch it up like the automobile version of Frankenstein. The finished product looked worse than before, with torn yellow foam spilling out of the monstrous holes, but we were proud of it.

Luckily, removing the staples was a simple process, and I didn't need any specific instructions. When I finished with the pillow, he said, "Good. Now come with me." He led me to the Bodell's home while I was still in my pajamas, and when we entered the home, Scott seemed just as bewildered at my presence as I was. That's when my dad handed me the staple remover.

"Has she done this before?" he asked.

"Oh yeah!" my dad and I assured him together. We left out the part where my "experience" was from five minutes prior on a pillow. As I removed the staples, the man kept a stoic silence, but another tear escaped, creeping down his cheek. When I finished, the couple thanked us, and, as the door closed behind us, my dad gave me a big pat on the back.

My dad put his surgical skills to good use each year at the 4-H and FFA turkey show. After my sister and I fattened up our flock and miraculously kept them from drowning in our kiddy pool that only had three inches of water in it, we took our prized gobblers to the processing plant where each contestant had their birds butchered. The last step in the process is a machine that removes the feathers, but it was rough and consistently nicked holes in the skin. The plumpness of those butterballs is only half the battle at a show. Presentation is everything, even in matters with the plucking machine, which the kids had no control over. Rips in the skin are left alone since the contestants don't know how to fix them, but my dad pulled out a suturing kit and gave

Alyssa and my birds the stitching equivalent of a Rembrandt. The holes disappeared.

He then went to every other child's bird and stitched them up with the same care and attention he had with ours. When the birds were lined up along the auction barn's forty-foot judging table, and we sat in stands huddled under heating lamps, we prepared for the moment of truth. The judge walked down the lineup of Thanksgiving-ready turkeys and carefully inspected each one. Motioning for the microphone, he announced to the crowd how impressed he was with the impeccably done skin repairs. Every kid there was beaming a little brighter that day.

24

A Daughter's Hero

The day of my father's retirement was unexpected. About a month before his scheduled farewell, he came home one afternoon and said he couldn't do it anymore. His passion was there, but his body was failing. Whenever he attempted to stitch up a laceration, his hands would shake enough to scare both him and his patients. He had also been working twelve-hour shifts long after his energy was spent. After hanging up his white coat, he made an appointment with his own doctor and heard the words he was dreading—Parkinson's disease. The doctor predicted he had already been living with it for the previous ten years.

Parkinson's directly affects nearly every aspect of his body and mind. Motor function is now limited, and some days it takes an extra effort to maintain his natural optimism. Thankfully, it has yet to take his wit and humor. My mother is an invaluable help, but on one occasion, I backed him up when he tried to sneak out of his daily exercise, telling her he had completed his thirty minutes after only doing six. I sat back, smiling as a witness, so he could get back to telling me more stories.

If there's one thing my dad has taught me, it's that we can't be afraid to laugh at our mistakes and that life is richer when we make peace with what makes us human. Shortly after his retirement, I came to visit and saw him perched on his hobby farm-sized John Deere tractor. He was sitting in the gravel driveway next to a hole and sporting a big grin. He explained that he'd been digging, for something I can't recall, when he accidentally hit both the water and electrical lines. He was now waiting for a plumber and an electrical technician to come to the rescue.

"I followed the proper protocol and called the 811 number to be sure where the lines were buried before digging," he said. "But when I dug the hole, guess where the lines were?"

"Where?" I asked.

"Right where they said they'd be!"

During high school, my sister regularly drove our parent's blue F-350 truck and, on her way home one afternoon, she made a stop for a fountain Coke at Sonic. There was construction on Main Street, and cones were lined up along the curb, but they were far apart, and she couldn't tell where the entrance was. The burger joint was still open, apparent from the customer cars in the parking lot, so she headed for what she thought was the entrance and pulled in. As she slipped between the markers, the truck plowed right into wet cement. "Oh crap," she said. A construction worker hurried over, shaking his head, and Alyssa could see his expression say, "I'm getting fired for this."

The city was forced to close down Main Street and bring a crane in to pull the truck out. As soon as she was free, she beelined it for the car wash and gave the truck a deep cleaning. When she got home, our dad wasn't upset at all. In fact, the only thing he gave her a hard time about was why her boyfriend, who had been with her, didn't get a picture.

When my husband called me one evening and told me he had been in a minor car accident but was unharmed, he worried I would be upset that my favorite car now had a crumpled hole in the bumper. I suppose it was my dad coming out of my mouth when I said, "I'll just put a sticker over it. It'll probably look better than it did before." A few weeks later, I accidentally backed my husband's car into a trailer hitch and put a dent in his bumper. He wasn't bothered either, but I cut out a paper heart and taped it over the top.

As a teenager, I had a vast array of emotions and a plethora of struggles in my attempt to navigate high school. Whenever I had a problem, I waited until our family was in bed and all the lights in the house were out before creeping out of my room and tiptoeing to the living room. I knew my dad would be awake, a familiarity confirmed by the quiet voices coming from the TV. Following the glow of "Walker, Texas Ranger," I silently inched into the living room where he smiled and welcomed me in. No matter what I had to say or how long I talked, he listened. I knew those nights meant a lot of lost sleep, but he never let me believe he would have it any other way. Those late nights were my saving grace, and he made sure if something was important to my sister or me, it was important to him.

He was a very hands-on parent, and every Friday night during those teenage years, he threw burgers on the grill for Alyssa and my friends. We played night games, including an advanced form of hide-and-go-seek tag where we had the run of the property and could hide anywhere in the barn or the three other outbuildings. I liked climbing onto the roof of the old chicken coop, now used as a doghouse for the Great Danes, and tucked myself into the shadows where the moon's glow couldn't find me. I didn't know then, but those burgers were the lure to encourage our friends to be at our house so he could keep a watchful eye.

Apart from his protective nature, he was also very trusting. Alyssa and I had made some poor decisions like any other teenager, but we were good kids, and he gave us a lot of credit for that. On one cold, winter evening, Alyssa and I had been out on the town with friends and had played musical chairs with our cars. Somehow our friend, Brad, ended up driving my dad's white Corolla, but our mistake was letting him go alone with no map or phone to contact us. He had recently driven in from Georgia to attend college and was completely unfamiliar with the area. As you can imagine, we quickly lost him, and now it was dark and snowing. Since we had no way of communicating with him, the best idea I could come up with was to stand on the corner of Main Street and hope he drove by and saw me. Remarkably, he managed to find his way back to my house, despite being ten miles away and only having been there once before.

My dad was watching out the kitchen window when his Corolla pulled into the driveway. He was puzzled that my sister and I weren't in it, and instead, saw a stranger. Nonetheless, he welcomed Brad with a big handshake and didn't seem bothered that this stranger couldn't tell him where his daughters were. They sat and chatted until the rest of us gave up searching in town and headed back to the house to see if he had tried returning there.

I was beyond relieved to find both the car and my friend safe, not to mention grateful my dad was not bothered by the mishap. Years later, Brad and I would get married, and my parents welcomed him with open arms. He often reminds me of my dad with his wit and humor, and I see him every time Brad turns his ballcap backward. The subtle act takes me back to the days when my dad and I would be standing atop a mountain slope and ready to push off down the hill, because that was the moment my dad would turn his hat around, preventing it from being blown off by the rushing wind.

Of all the characteristics my dad and I had hoped my future husband would have, Brad infringed on one of them. When I was in ninth grade, I had written up a list and where one question asked, "Career," and I wrote, "Anything except business." My dad instilled in me that owning a business was a sinking ship and used his experience with MEPCO as evidence. When I asked him why he had struggled with MEPCO, his answer had always been, "I'm just not a businessman." It wasn't until Brad asked the same question that he gave the full answer. "I didn't just pour the company's profits into top-fuel racing. I poured everything in," he said.

When asked if he had a fatherly role model whom he looked up to for an example, his answer was Dr. Cliff Huxtable from "The Cosby Show." He said, "I admired how loving of a father he was and how attentive he was with his children. He was the example I needed, someone who could be a great father and doctor at the same time." My dad's persistent optimism also taught me I could be anything I wanted if I worked hard enough, not just by his words but also by the way he lived his life. His stories filled me with awe and taught me that life isn't meant to be endured but seized and made the most of. A little bit of him showed through me the day I decided to mix Tannerite explosives with gasoline and told my daughters to watch because it was going to be a blast, pun intended. When we were younger, he used to take my sister and me through the car wash and would wait until the strongest water nozzles were pounding the glass by our faces and then drop our windows down. He would roar with laughter while we screamed in a mixture of excitement and horror, but when it was over, we couldn't wait to do it again.

Easily demonstrated in his academic and personal life, he loved learning. School tests were a thrilling challenge, and he told me I didn't need to fear them if I studied hard enough and was prepared. I soon found I had inherited the same passion for learning, doing well in school, and constantly finding new things to teach myself at home. My education didn't end when I graduated as I continued to feast on books that told the stories of brave men and women who overcame incredible odds. My husband chuckles every time I find a new hobby to learn, whether it's cake decorating or making wet specimens by putting a dead rat in a jar of formaldehyde.

Not all my dad's ventures proved successful, but it never stopped him from trying new things. Throughout his time in jr. high and high school, he joined several sports teams, but each one failed. On the football team, his coach had to constantly remind him to stop tackling the wrong people, along with a myriad of other rule violations. "I wasn't getting flagged on purpose. I just didn't know any better," he said. He then tried his luck on the wrestling team, only to find he wasn't any better at it than football. When his persistence didn't work, he attempted to enter a lower weight class by losing weight on a grapefruit-only diet that his grandmother frowned upon. Once he made it to the lower weight class, he found out he was just as lousy there too.

I knew my dad would support me in whatever I chose to do with my life, although the day I called home from college with the idea of dropping out to attend cosmetology school was not met with the same enthusiasm. The idea came to me not because I was fascinated with the career but because I thought I could make money by cutting the neighbor's hair from my future home. My parents didn't stop me, but they gave me a good, "You better sleep on that."

He continually showered my sister and me in praise, making me want to be the person he already seemed to think I was. Now with a family of my own, I realize that hasn't changed, and I continue wanting to make him proud in everything I do. He is the mirror that sees the best in me, and I know he will forever be my greatest supporter. For everything he did in life, somehow, he believes I can do more.

I pass on my dad's stories each night to my girls, who regularly beg, "Please tell us another story about Grandpa!" When I look into their eyes, I see the same wide-eyed fascination I had when he would tell me. As I wrote this book, I enjoyed countless hours back in his living room, sitting across from him and listening as he re-told them for me. We spent more time laughing than anything else, and no matter what my meager writing skills may produce, I will treasure that time forever. More than recording old stories, I learned new ones and got to know him as more than just my father. With the help and contributions of what seems like a village, I hope this book lives up to his legacy and preserves his story for generations.

Whenever I visit, if my dad isn't on the lawnmower, he's stretched out on the couch drinking a glass of Chardonnay from a cardboard box and watching B-rated movies, like *Sharknado* and *Mega Shark vs. Crocosaurus*. He and I share an affinity for sci-fi and monster movies, but for me, the more money that's thrown into a film, the better. On the latest visit, my mom walked in to check on us, and he made a cheeky comment to her and threw me a grin. Finding new ways to make her eyes roll is one of his favorite activities. When the movie ended and he headed outside for some fresh air, he paused by the front door and turned to me.

"Do you know what the best feeling is?"

"No, what?" I asked.

"A sticky doorknob. It means there are grandkids around."

"Thanks for looking on the bright side, Dad," I said and apologized for not being more diligent with my kids and their sticky mitts.

"I'm not kiddin' ya," he replied, and as he stared out the window, I could see a genuine smile.

ACKNOWLEDGEMENTS

This book would not have been possible without my dad and the countless hours he spent retelling these stories for me. I will cherish every moment on that couch, laughing and making new memories as we relived old ones. My mother was usually there laughing alongside us and contributing invaluable details. Thank you, Mom.

Much of the depth and detail are owed to the kindness of my dad's old buddies and lifelong friends, who took the time to send me stories and answer questions. I feel like this book was written by a village, and in many ways, it was. It was fun to hear my dad's stories from other perspectives and see him through their eyes. With their help, I was able to paint a more thorough picture, both of my dad and the adventures they shared.

From Alta, I would like to thank Stuart Thompson, Darwon Stoneman, Hamilton George Strayer III "Hambone," Bruce Remington, Court Richards, Bentsen Moss, and "Hook" Ershler. However, the two patrolmen I'd like to give extra appreciation to are Doug Christenson, who took the time to read the manuscript, fill in details, and correct inaccuracies, as well as Bill Binger, for contributing several stories, including those from his own book, *210 to Alta*.

ACKNOWLEDGEMENTS

To Jack Walker, for your invaluable perspective, and for being the best friend my dad could ask for. Thank you to Humberto and your family for bringing many of these stories to life and for trusting us with your daughters as they pursued educational opportunities in the US. We have enjoyed swapping stories about our fathers. Thank you to the rest of the neurosurgery department at Primary Children's, especially Anitsa Aiello and Patty Mavor.

I wish to give a heartfelt thank you to the families who contributed their own stories to this book. To the Gowans family for allowing me to share Brian's story, and for every one of the million ways your family has blessed ours. To Barbara and Delbert Ross for letting me share your adversity on Lake Powell. To our dear friends, Scott and Madeleine Murdock, thank you for contributing warm tales of my dad and for allowing me to share Stan's story. He was truly a man among men, and will forever be missed.

Thank you to Scott and Jolene Droubay for sharing your stories, especially the rescue at Lake Powell and being the first to rush to their aid. Thank you to Linda Nelson for sharing your experiences scuba diving with my dad and for mentoring three generations of my family. To Neal Farwell, for sharing wonderful details from your time with my dad in Naval basic training.

I wish to send a thank you to my grandmother, Colleen, in Heaven. She passed away before I began writing this book, but somehow, she knew what I needed and gave it to me years ago. When I found her writings, I cried because it was exactly what I needed when I knew I had lost my chance to ask her. I love you, Grandma.

ACKNOWLEDGEMENTS

Thank you to my uncle Chris Carter for sharing his childhood memories with my dad and helping track down old information. To my Grandpa Don for sharing stories about hunting with my dad when he was twelve, and how his idea of "getting some firewood" was cutting down every dead tree in the area. To my uncle, Mark, and my dad's uncles, George and Bruce Fisher, thank you for sharing your stories, especially about my dad during his youth.

A big thanks to Molly Daniel, for taking the time to edit this book, and giving me wise advice in its development. You helped me find the right questions to ask and gave me the feedback I needed. To Parker Boggess for letting me take a picture of your sweet Jeep for the cover of this book. To Jason Staheli for traveling down in your scrubs to take a picture in front of that Jeep, posing as a stand-in for my dad. You probably didn't have any modeling experience, but you nailed it. I know I didn't need a real Physician Assistant for the photo, but that just made you a hundred times better.

A HUGE thank you to my husband, Brad, for supporting me and making it possible to pour an entire year into this project. I apologize for all the dinners I didn't make because I was engulfed in another writing marathon. Lucky for the kids, you're a better cook than I am. Also, thank you for letting me fly out with the kids and spend weeks at a time in Utah so I could be with my dad. You were the first person who told me I could write a book and helped me find the classes that would teach me. I wouldn't be the woman I am today without you.

As a last expression of gratitude, I want to thank my dad for teaching me that life does not have limits and that the greatest

ACKNOWLEDGEMENTS

thing we can do is serve others. Thank you for making this world a better place. You have touched countless lives and that effect will be felt for generations. Most of all, thank you for being the dad every little girl dreams of. You were there when we needed you, plus every moment since. Thank you for making Alyssa and I feel like the most loved daughters in the world.

About the Author

Brichelle is a mother of three daughters, whom she loves sharing stories of her father with. She is a passionate reader of history and personal memoirs of survival. As a Utah native, she now resides in Georgia, but returns regularly to spend time with her parents, twin sister, and the snow. She loves living in the countryside, raising goats and chickens, and eating cookie dough. When she isn't eating a shameful amount of chocolate, she's jumping into the next creative project and taking her girls with her.

Brichelle with her husband, Brad

Lightning Source UK Ltd.
Milton Keynes UK
UKHW010029250522
403484UK00003B/57